Airline Pilot Technical Interviews

A Study Guide

By
Ronald D. McElroy

Airline Pilot Technical Interviews: A Study Guide
Ronald D. McElroy
Cover Design by Benson Communications
Editing and Layout by Pam Ryan
Copyright 1999 by Ronald D. McElroy,Copyright 1999 on "Staying the
Course" by Cheryl A. Cage
Second Printing 2001

Printed in the United States of America
Published by CAGE CONSULTING, INC.

Library of Congress Catalog Card Number: 98-074575

ISBN 0-9642839-4-8

Disclaimer: This book is sold with the understanding that the publisher
and the author are not engaged in rendering legal services. If legal
expert assistance is required, the services of a competent professional
should be sought.

This book is a general information book on how to prepare for a
professional pilot technical interview. It is understood that the
information contained in this book does not guarantee success. The
author and publisher shall have neither liability nor responsibility to
any person or entity with respect to any loss or damage caused, or
alleged to be caused directly or indirectly by the information contained
in this book.

The reader accepts complete responsibility for the accuracy of the
information they provide during an interview. If you do not wish to be
bound by the above, you may return this book to the publisher for a full
refund.

Table of Contents

INTRODUCTION

The decision to write this study guide stemmed from a couple of very simple and natural ideas.

For the past year I had been conducting technical mock interviews for Cheryl Cage. The reception and feedback was overwhelmingly positive. My first goal was to capture in writing the process and information that I had been presenting during these technical mock interviews with Cage Consulting.

Second, I had worked hard to polish my natural teaching ability through the many years of flight and ground instruction of new and seasoned pilots. The knowledge was already in place from years of repetition in the classrooms and briefing rooms plus line flying. I just had to get my knowledge on paper. I felt confident the words would flow easily to the keyboard.

I hope you enjoy my presentation of the material. But, more important, I hope by the time you finish this book you will be able to more easily review and grasp the subjects discussed. Not only will your reviews ensure better performance during a technical interview or test, but I hope you learn something new that will help you fly the line a little better.

A NOTE FROM THE PUBLISHER

Even though I have been in the business of assisting pilots with preparing for the airline interviewing process since 1988 it still never ceases to amaze me how much dedication and planning is needed to secure, and maintain, a smooth professional pilot career. For this reason we are constantly looking for new products and services to assist our pilot clients preparing for their highest career goals.

Toward this end we began offering Technical Practice Study Groups. To find the best people to teach these study groups I asked pilot friends who worked in the training departments of various major airlines for recommendations of individuals who might fit my stringent requirements. Out of the numerous pilots I interviewed, I hired two. One of those pilots was Ron McElroy.

Over the course of the next year I became more and more impressed with not only Ron's technical knowledge, but with his obvious passion for teaching, and his unwavering desire to help our clients succeed.

I approached Ron about writing a technical interview study guide. He immediately said yes. And, within two months, presented me with the manuscript for *Airline Pilot Technical Interviews*.

Airline Pilot Technical Interviews was written for two reasons: to help the pilot applicant prioritize the areas which need to be reviewed, and to offer inventive and easy-to-use tips on maintaining your focus no matter what types of questions are being asked.

I am proud to be the publisher of this excellent study guide. I know you will enjoy and appreciate the remarkable job Ron has done in presenting the information you will need to score high marks in your technical interviews.

Good luck!

Cheryl A. Cage
President
Cage Consulting, Inc

Chapter I

RISING TO THE CHALLENGE

Hey—you made it! You've been accumulating hours and have made the decision to charge ahead toward the airline career you've sacrificed for. No matter what your professional level, you feel ready to break into the ranks of the regionals or the major airlines. Whatever your **immediate** goals, you are ready to start preparing for the airline interviewing process. Congratulations!

But wait! Are you really ready? No matter what your background, your education, or your aviation experience, there's always room for a little extra wisdom and knowledge to help you ultimately land that mega-million dollar, major airline career.

Not to worry! Getting that extra wisdom and knowledge is part of my job and my promise to you: if you make a commitment to focus on the right stuff-which I'll feature here in this study guide-you will be as ready as you can possibly be for the technical part of any airline interview process.

Please understand that as we go through *Airline Pilot Technical Interviews*, I am making the assumption that you are current and actively flying airplanes and that you have a grasp of basic math and science concepts and formulas including aerodynamics. As such, this guide will make reference to the materials that all of us studied in the past while preparing for our commercial, flight instructor, multi-engine, instrument, ATP, flight engineer, and type ratings.

Here's what I recommend for your personal library to prepare you for the airline technical interview:

- ***Aeronautical Information Manual (AIM)***. Make sure it contains the latest revisions. Available through aviation bookstores and the Government Printing Office (GPO).

- ***Federal Aviation Regulations (FAR)*** to include Parts 1, 61, and 91 as a minimum. Pilots current in Part 121/135 air carrier operations, or that possess an Airline Transport Pilot certificate, will be expected to be knowledgeable in the appropriate sections. Available through aviation bookstores and the GPO.

- *Aviation Weather, Advisory Circular 00-6A,* published jointly by the FAA and the National Weather Service. Available at aviation bookstores and the GPO.

- *Airline Transport Pilot (ATP) Test Prep.* A study guide for the FAA written test. Available through aviation bookstores.

- *Flight Engineer (FEX) Test Prep.* A study guide for the FAA written test. Available through aviation bookstores.

- *Checklist for Success: A Pilot's Guide to the Successful Airline Interview* by Cheryl A. Cage. (Book and interactive CD) A guide to understanding and preparing for the competitive professional pilot interviews. Available by calling 1-888-899-CAGE or ordering online through www.cageconsulting.com

*A special note: You must ensure that all test preps, regulations, and AIM are up to date. These references are quickly outdated. **You must have** the latest revisions—it will save you an embarrassing moment at the interviews!*

How much time should you dedicate to this technical interview preparation? Your study habits determine that answer, but let me suggest the following:

AIM	10 hours
FARs	10 hours
Approach plates	2 hours
Enroute charts	1 hour
Aviation weather	2 hours
Current aircraft systems, limits, and procedures	2 hours
Basic aerodynamics	2 hours
Company OPSPECs or military flight regulations	1 hour
Airline Pilot Technical Interviews	30 hours
ATP Test Prep	5 hours
FEX Test Prep	5 hours
TOTAL	70 hours

This study plan assumes that you are current and flying and only need to brush up on these subject areas. If you've been away from active flying for even a short time, if you consider yourself a "study-challenged" pilot, or if you are new to many of these subject areas (as a new pilot), plan on spending lots more time and definitely consider getting a tutor or mentor. But, as I said earlier, this study guide will help you focus on the right stuff and steer you in the right direction for your studies.

Just to be clear, this study guide contains all of the study areas that, based on Cage Consulting's work with pilot applicants, are being used for the technical interviews or testing. As such, this study guide may not be as comprehensive as those you used to study for the commercial, instrument, or ATP certificates. So, don't be alarmed at the brevity of the explanations. My primary goal is to review and teach you what you will need to shine in the **technical** portion of the interview. Additional material is offered solely as a basis for background information to help support your understanding of the answer. If your airline interviewer uses a variation of the question, you'll be able to more easily adapt to the new content of the question and thereby figure out the answer.

Be aware that in your studies you may discover differences between your company operation specifications (OPSPECs) and the FARs, AIM, or my explanations in this study guide. Source documents from the FAA such as the FARs, AIM, and TERPs (United States Standard for Terminal Instrument Procedures) **always** supersede my explanations. And, of course, your company OPSPECs can be more restrictive (and sometimes out of date) for specific types of operations. My answers and explanations refer to the most current revisions available from government source documents.

The purpose of the additional personal study with your own library references that I mentioned is to ensure that you have a broad enough understanding to avoid even the appearance of being spoon-fed the answers and the resulting lack of confidence when presented with a question that has been slightly varied from the questions you'll see here.

There are three additional areas of preparation that I strongly encourage, yet I will not be able to adequately cover them in this guide. They include a thorough study and understanding of the flight manual of your current airplane, independent study and review of approach plates and enroute charts with an emphasis on understanding the legend and symbols, and a commitment to schedule a mock interview with qualified and competent airline consultants. **This last step will give you the confidence to excel at the most important interview ever!**

Imagine yourself getting that prize-winning envelope today in the mail with the return address showing the logo of the airline of your dreams! Hurrah! Yes, they've invited you in for the interview. But wait—it's a week from today—and you have a trip to fly between now and then. **Don't wait to prepare. Start now!** Information gained in last minute cram courses has a way of deserting you when you need it most. **I repeat. Don't wait until the last minute!** That means starting your personal study, scheduling the mock interview well in advance, and showing up in plenty of time and prepared for the mock interview. Trust me when I tell you that a pilot who is not prepared for the interview, just as in flying, is easy to spot. Don't be that unprepared pilot.

So, what do you think? Is 70 hours of prep time worth it? Consider this: if this airline job of your dreams were to put an additional two to five million dollars into your paycheck and pension over the next 15 to 30 years, would that make a difference to you? That's a "paycheck" of $70,000 per study hour!

Well, that's as good a flight plan I can give you. It's up to you to get started and get airborne.

Study well. Good Luck!

Ronald D. McElroy

NOTES

Chapter 2

MENTAL MATH METHODS

Reciprocal Headings

Seems a simple enough problem—yet, in the heat of battle you may freeze if you haven't practiced.

Only two approaches seem appropriate to get through this question: use a formula or visualize the headings on a compass rose.

Let's set up a practice table and work on using the formula.

Initial Heading	Reciprocal Heading
090	270
011	191
222	042
355	175
167	347
313	133

Use this formula:

Init Hdg + 200° - 20° = Recip Hdg

(When smaller than 180°)

or

Init Hdg - 200° + 20° = Recip Hdg

(When greater than 180°)

Notice the change of the plus and minus signs between the formulas. The reason for the two formulas is to work with initial headings either smaller than 180° or greater than 180° to begin the formula.

For example:

090° + 200° - 20° = 270°

or

222° - 200° + 20° = 042°

Be cautious in using this formula for certain ranges of headings that will initially give you an answer that is either greater than 360° or less than zero in the first step of adding or subtracting the 200.

After completing the second step of subtracting or adding the 20, your answer will be corrected back into the appropriate range of 001^0 to 360^0. Also, don't forget that the last digit always remains the same when computing the reciprocal.

For example:

$$167° + 200° - 20° = 347°$$

or

$$191° - 200° + 20° = 011°$$

The second approach to figuring reciprocal headings using the compass rose comes simply with experience in flying on instruments. Rather than spend a lot of time with the theories of IFR flying, I recommend that you practice these reciprocals the next time you go fly. I believe you'll find it very productive and easier the more you work on it.

Illustration 1: Heading Indicator

Temperature Conversions

Here are a couple of shortcuts to quickly convert Fahrenheit to Celsius and back again. It's important to memorize just a few important points, then use the tools to figure a rough estimate of the conversion. Here are the formulas, followed by a short table showing a couple of memorable temperature points:

$$°F = [(9/5) \times °C] + 32$$

$$°C = [°F - 32] \times (5/9)$$

Celsius	Fahrenheit
0°	32°
15°	59°
30°	86°
40°	104°

I chose 15° C and 59° F on the table as this is the temperature for a standard atmospheric day at sea level.

Some pilots are at ease using the conversion formulas. Perhaps they use it a lot; for me, I need a gimmick. Let me explain three techniques.

First, if we note from the table above that the freezing temperature of water at 0°C equals 32°F, simply add or subtract 5 degrees Celsius for each 9 degrees Fahrenheit or vice versa.

For example, let's figure what 30 degrees Celsius is in Fahrenheit. Remembering that there are 5°C for each 9°F, 30°C is the same as (6x5°C) and 30°C is really O°+30°C. Now take the 6 (from 6x5°C) and multiply it by 9°F (6x9°F=54) and add that result to 32°F. Remember 0°C=32°F, getting 54°F+32°F=86°F.

It's relatively easy to use this 5 equals 9 or 9 equals 5 matching as long as you know just a few markers along the way. Try a couple of problems on your own, they're simple enough to catch on quickly.

The second technique is to double the °C, subtract 10%, and add 32. Or, subtract 32 from the °F, add 10% and divide the result by two. This is not very difficult and results in much more accuracy.

```
[(°C x 2) - 10%] + 32 = °F

[(°F - 32) + 10%] ÷ 2 = °C
```

The third way of estimating will get you in the ballpark for **lower** temperatures. Either double the °C and add 30 to get °F, or subtract 30 from the °F and cut that in half to get °C.

```
(2 x °C) + 30 = °F

(°F - 30) ÷ 2 = °C
```

What's the Pressure Altitude?

Sitting in the cockpit, if you set 29.92 in. Hg in your barometric altimeter, you would then be reading the standard day pressure altitude for your location. Simple enough, right?

Now, a problem may occur when you must figure your pressure altitude based on a particular altimeter setting other than standard and using your local airport elevation.

This, again, is quite simple. For every .01 in. Hg altimeter setting, your pressure altitude reading changes 10 feet.

*The ATIS altimeter setting (QNH) is 29.79
in. Hg and the local airport elevation is
460' MSL. What is the pressure altitude?*

?
.

Answer: Pressure altitude equals 590 feet.
The difference between 29.79 in. Hg and 29.92 in.
Hg is .13 inches which converts to a difference of
130 feet pressure altitude. Since we need to add the
.13 in. Hg to 29.79 in. Hg to equal the standardized
29.92 in. Hg, we also add the 130' to the airport
elevation of 460' to figure the pressure altitude.

Crosswind Components

In position and holding for takeoff, or on
short final for an approach, ATC gives you airport
winds that seem a little strong and at a funny angle.
How can you figure the crosswind component in a
hurry to ensure you operate within the flight manual
limitations?

Here's a quick technique I picked up that does an okay job of figuring a rough crosswind component. I'll explain with the use of a small table. I have provided three ways of using the multiplier in the right column, depending on your personal preference.

Wind Angle to Runway	Calculated Crosswind Component		
0 or 180	0.0	0%	None
030 or 150	0.5	50%	Half
045 or 135	0.7	70%	Two-thirds
060 or 120	0.9	90%	Almost all
090	1.0	100%	All

Please understand, these are rough estimates only and not necessarily mathematically exact. Close enough, though, for a quick look-see.

To use this technique/table, first you have to determine the angular difference between the runway heading and the direction of the winds that ATC is providing you. Second, choose one of the closer "angles" from the table. Third, use the multiplier from the right column with the total wind value, including gust. Let's do a couple of quick problems. Just fill in the blank.

Wind Angle to Runway	Total Wind Strength	Crosswind Component
030	20	?
050	20	?
070	18	?

As a quick check, using the table above, the answers I would have come up with are 10, 14, and 16 knots of crosswind component respectively. Your answers could vary slightly if you rounded off differently than I did. The key element here, for me, is to find a simple "crutch" that's easy to use in the cockpit when you are otherwise very busy.

Now, can you make the same crosswind calculation if the winds are between 090 and 180 degrees offset from the runway? Sure. Using the same table, the crosswind components for 120, 135, and 150 degrees offset match up with 060, 045, and 030 degrees, respectively, on the table.

Visibility to RVR Conversions

Visibility to RVR conversions do not have a linear relationship. Remember that visibility is given in statute miles and runway visual range is given in feet. My suggestion is that you memorize this short conversion table.

Visibility	RVR
1/4 Statute Mile	1,600 feet
1/2 Statute Mile	2,400 feet
3/4 Statute Mile	4,000 feet
1 Statute Mile	5,000 feet
1 1/4 Statute Mile	6,000 feet

Time / Speed / Distance Problems

This is the one subject that I've noticed with interviewees that seems to show that either the light bulb is burning brightly or is obviously dimmed through years of neglect. Perhaps I can knock the dust out of the inner chambers with a few techniques.

First, remember that there will be only four variables in the formula, and the interviewer will need to give you three of them. These four are **wind, distance, time**, and **true airspeed.**

Second, I've found it helpful, after hearing the three numbers, to immediately convert the speed (if given) into miles per minute. Say again? That's right, it seems to be easier to solve most problems when you know how many miles per minute you are traveling.

If you don't have a good grasp of converting knots to miles per minute, study this chart and memorize the relationships, even the half mile per minute numbers. Trust me, cramming this chart into your memory just to pass a couple of math problems will be well worth the effort.

Ground Speed-Knots*	Miles per Minute
60	1
90	1.5
120	2
150	2.5
180	3
210	3.5
240	4
270	4.5
300	5
330	5.5
360	6
390	6.5
420	7
450	7.5
480	8
510	8.5
540	9

*Note: Feedback from prior interviewees is that no one has been asked to figure the wind variable. If it's not given to you, assume it to be zero.

As an additional crutch, remember, every 30 knots equals .5 miles/minute, or 60 knots equals 1 mile/minute. You can then quickly figure that, for example, 480 knots = 8 miles/minute.

The basic time-speed-distance formula is this:

$$(GS) \times (Time) = (Distance)$$

The speed variable in the formula refers to ground speed. Therefore, **you must add or subtract the head wind or tailwind component to the true airspeed to get the ground speed in knots.**

```
TAS +/- Wind = GS
```

Here's a table of problems containing four variables. Three are given to you, leaving the fourth for you to solve. Answers will be shown on the next page.

KTAS	Headwind (HW) Tailwind (TW)	Time	Distance
240	60 TW	?	200 NM
280	70 HW	10 min.	?
150	0	?	5 NM
?	0	4	20 NM
420	60 TW	?	400 NM
?	0	2 min.	14 NM
?	0	1.5 hr.	600 NM
500	0	45 min.	?
?	0	40 min.	340 NM

Here's how to use my technique of converting ground speed to miles per minute to make the problem solving easier during the interview. Simplicity is critical since it is very rare that you are allowed a calculator or pad and pencil to work the formula.

First, as soon as you are given the ground speed, or can figure it out from the true airspeed and winds, convert that to miles per minute.
EXAMPLE: 350 knots GS = 360 divided by 60 = 6mpm (notice that 350 is close enough to 360 to use because it is an exact multiple of 60 (knots = 1 mpm).

Second, you can then more easily multiply this miles per minute by the number of minutes to get the distance traveled. Or, you can divide the distance by the miles per minute to figure the number of minutes. For example:

```
10 minutes @ 6 mpm = 60 miles
```

or

```
90 miles @ 6 mpm = 15 minutes.
```

Feedback from candidates has been that the problems have relatively easy numbers to work with   no complex fractions or huge numbers. The one exception is having the half mile per minute increment in the ground speed.

Here are the answers to the table of problems on the previous page.

KTAS	Headwind (HW) Tailwind (TW)	Time	Distance
240	60 TW	40 min	200 NM
280	70 HW	10 min.	35 NM
150	0	2 min.	5 NM
300	0	4 min.	20 NM
420	60 TW	50 min.	400 NM
420	0	2 min.	14 NM
400	0	1.5 hr.	600 NM
500	0	45 min.	375 NM
510	0	40 min.	340 NM

Notice the last three problems were more easily solved by using an approach of proportions. That is, if you realize that 1.5 hour is three segments of 0.5 hours, and that 600 NM is three segments of 200 NM, then you realize that you travel 200 NM per half-hour or 400 NM per hour. Thus, 400 knots ground speed.

Next, realizing 45 minutes is three segments of 15 minutes, and that 500 knots is a distance of 250 NM each 30 minutes or 125 NM each 15 minutes, then, three segments of the 125 NM per 15 minutes equals 375 NM in 45 minutes.

Finally, in the last problem, one easy approach to figure the GS is to recognize that since you've traveled 340 NM in 40 minutes you would also travel 170 NM in 20 (divide both variables by 2), and then multiply both of these by a factor of 3 which results in traveling 510 NM (170 x 3) in 60 minutes (20 x 3) or one hour.

Let me emphasize that during an interview it is critical that you listen intently to the numbers that are given to you. Develop a habit during your practice of these problems to sequentially memorize three numbers. Knowing the formula from above, the most variables they can give you is three, leaving the fourth for you to solve. If you are not able to capture all of the numbers the first time around, you have no choice but to ask that they be repeated. I also recommend that once the numbers are given to you to solve that you repeat them back to the interviewer just to confirm that what you heard was correct and to reinforce your memory of the numbers.

Also, some people find it helpful to verbalize their problem solving out loud. I agree with this technique, **if you believe this will help you to be more methodical.** Be careful, however, since any blundering of the numbers out loud could be even more embarrassing!

In addition, please remember that the questions will probably all have numbers that show relationships that are somewhat simple to work with even if the numbers are large; i.e., the questions will be designed to allow you to work them in your head if you understand them and will not require a calculator or scratch pad and pen.

Having said this, could you repeat solving the problems in the table with a little more ease and confidence? If not, keep trying till you can. It's worth the effort!

There is one higher level problem that has been asked by the airlines only a few times that I know of. It involves one additional step. Let me paraphrase the question:

You are cruising at FL 310 at 540 knots ground speed. You have been cleared to descend to 16,000 feet, and you know your aircraft will average 3,000 fpm during the descent. How far will you travel during the descent?

Here's how I would set it up to solve the problem in my head. Again, I would need to intently focus on the numbers for a few seconds to anchor them in my short term memory.

First, my speed at 540 knots is 9 nautical miles per minute.

Second, I need to descend 15,000 feet at an average rate of 3,000 fpm which gives me 5 minutes to descend.

Third, to find the distance traveled, I multiply (9 NM/min.) x (5 min.) which equals 45 NM.

Fuel Dump Problems

These tend to be easier problems to work in your head because there are usually only three variables (dump rate, time, fuel dumped) to work with in the formula. Two of the three will be given to you, leaving you to discover the third variable.

The greater challenge in this problem is working with large numbers, probably in the thousands of pounds. But, don't get too anxious, the problems are normally designed so that the answers work out in round numbers. And, better yet, many of the questions I've heard of ask you to solve the time variable. Therefore, your practice of these problems can be more methodical and consistent.

(Fuel Dumped) / (Dump Rate) = (Time)

or

(Dump rate) x (Time) = (Fuel Dumped)

Here's a table of problems for you to practice with.

Dump Rate	Time	Fuel Dumped
1,300 ppm	?	6,500 lb.
2,500 ppm	?	45,000 lb.
3,000 ppm	?	19,000 lb.
2,500 ppm	?	30,000 lb.
2,200 ppm	?	11,000 lb.
1,500 ppm	7 min.	?
1,200 ppm	11 min.	?
?	5 min.	12,500 lb.
?	16 min.	48,000 lb.
2,000 ppm	?	20,000 lb.

It will be much simpler if you remember to drop two zeros from the end of each number just to keep the numbers more manageable in size rather than outrageously large.

Next, use one of two approaches to divide the Fuel Dumped by the Dump Rate. Using the first technique on the first problem, you would divide 65 by 13 (after dropping the last two zeroes) which equals 5 minutes. This method is strictly a mathematical approach that some can readily calculate in their head.

The other technique is to use a method of proportions to arrive at the proper solution. In the second problem, using the numbers 25 and 450 I would first double the dump rate to 50 so that I could more easily recognize that 450 divided by 50 equals nine; therefore, 450 divided by 25 equals 18 minutes.

Let's look again at the first problem using a variation on this technique. Using the numbers 13 and 65, I first double 13 to get 26 (a multiplier of 2). I then double 26 to get 52 (now a multiplier of 4). Then I recognize that I have a remainder of 13 (a multiplier of 1). Thus, I now have multipliers of 4 plus 1 which equals 5. This is the correct answer.

Let's do this again using problem three, using the numbers 3 and 19 (I can drop three zeroes in each number). I know that if I multiply 3 by 6 the result is 18 with a remainder of 1. What do I do with this? So far we know the answer is 6 minutes plus something. But, to be exact, we can see that the remainder of 1 divided by the dump rate of 3 equals one-third of a minute. Therefore, we now have an exact answer of 6 minutes and 20 seconds.

Here are the answers for the previous practice table:

Dump Rate	Time	Fuel Dumped
1,300 ppm	5 min.	6,500 lb.
2,500 ppm	18 min.	4,500 lb.
3,000 ppm	6 min. 20 sec.	19,000 lb.
2,500 ppm	12 min.	30,000 lb.
2,200 ppm	5 min.	11,000 lb.
1,500 ppm	7 min.	10,500 lb.
1,200 ppm	11 min.	13,200 lb.
2,500 ppm	5 min.	12,500 lb.
3,000 ppm	16 min.	48,000 lb.
2,000 ppm	10 min.	20,000 lb.

The 60 to 1 Rule

Remember this from your basic instrument course way back when? Well, I don't know specifically that any airline is quizzing you on this navigational tool, but it may help you get through other related problems on an approach plate or enroute chart. Here we go.

The 60 to 1 rule means that at 60 DME from a VOR every 1 degree of course deviation equals 1 nautical mile. Let me illustrate this in two formats.

First, a table:

DME from VOR	1 Degree = ? NM
60	1
30	½ or .50
20	1/3 or .33
15	1/4 or .25
12	1/5 or .20
10	1/6 or .16

Or, to use a formula:

```
# of Radials per mile = 60 / DME

Width of 1 degree (NM) = DME / 60
```

Pictorially, this 1 degree slice of pie in the sky looks like the following diagram. Perhaps it will better illustrate the relationships of the DME versus the distance per degree.

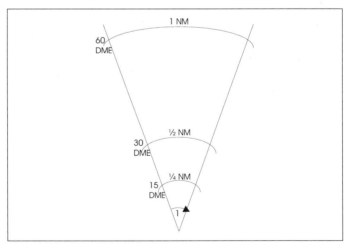

Illustration 2: 60 to 1 Rule

Here's a word problem to exercise the use of the 60 to 1 rule.

On the ILS 19R approach plate for XYZ airport, there is a 15 DME arc transition from the XYZ 047/15 (Sparky) to the XYZ 011/15 (Falfa). What is the distance along the arc from Sparky to Falfa?

Step one, calculate how many radials are crossed. 047 - 011 = 36 radials.

Step two, calculate the number of radials per nautical mile. 60 / 15 DME = 4 radials per nautical mile.

Step three, combine the answers from above to see that 36 radials divided by 4 radials/NM equals 9 NM. That's the answer.

One suggestion I have for simplification is to try always to use DMEs that make the formulas work out easily; i.e., if you are given 16 DME arc, use 15 DME instead.

Here's another word problem.

?

When flying the same ILS 19R transition using the 15 NM arc, how many degrees "lead" would you need to start the turn from the arc to the localizer, using standard rate turn at 200 knots? (Hint: SRT at 200 knots equals 30 degrees bank and 1 NM turn radius)

For practice change the above two practice problems to a 20 NM and 12 NM arc. Here are the answers:

DME Arc	Distance from Sparky to Falfa	Lead Radials from Arc to Localizer
15 NM	9 NM	4 degrees
20 NM	12 NM	3 degrees
12 NM	7.2 NM	5 degrees

Calculating Enroute Descents

Expect questions about calculating the distance required to descend from cruise altitude to a lower altitude crossing restriction. It is common in the industry to use a 3 to 1 ratio for calculating that distance.

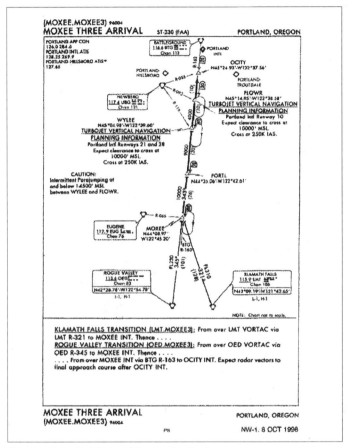

Illustration 3: Moxee Three Arrival

You are cruising at FL 270 and have been cleared to descend, pilot's discretion, to 12,000 feet by 12 DME before the next VOR. How far out would you start your descent?

The 3 to 1 rule means that you take the altitude (in 1,000s) you need to lose and multiply it by 3. This means we plan to fly 3 NM for every

1,000 feet of altitude lost. That's the distance required for most turbojet enroute descents at idle power. Here's how this problem works out:

Step one, figure out how much altitude there is to lose. In this case, it's 15,000 feet.

Step two, multiply the altitude (in 1,000s) to lose by a factor of 3, which is (15 x 3) = 45 NM.

Step three, compute the end of descent point, which is 12 DME. Add the enroute descent distance, which we just figured to be 45 NM, for a total of (12 + 45) = 57 DME before the next VOR to begin a normal enroute descent.

If your current aircraft uses a different formula to compute enroute descents, such as 2 or 2.5 times the altitude (in 1,000s), please use the factor for your aircraft rather than the 3 to 1 rule. The steps in the solution remain the same.

(Make sure the interviewer knows that you are calculating using your airplane's enroute descent forumla.)

Also consider the extra distance needed for a slowdown to comply with a crossing restriction. In the above example, if the cruise speed at FL 270 was 300 KIAS and the crossing restriction at 12,000 feet MSL included a slowdown to 250 KIAS, you would need to include an extra 1 NM per 10 knots to slow down, for a total extra distance of 5 NM. The final answer, therefore, would now be to start the enroute descent at 62 DME.

Let's now work a problem using a real world example.

Assume you are on a flight from San Jose to Portland, cruising at Flight Level 370 and 300 KIAS, and using the Klamath Falls transition to the Moxee Three Arrival. Referring to the Portland Moxee Three Arrival chart, calculate the start of an enroute descent based upon the following clearance.

"Flyways 777, you are cleared pilot's discretion to descend to cross Flowr intersection at 10,000 feet and 250 knots as published."

At what DME should you plan to start your enroute descent (no winds)?

Answer: You will need to start the descent 20 DME prior to Moxee.

Step one: You will need to descend 27,000 feet from FL370 to 10,000 MSL.

Step two: 27 x 3 = 81 NM to descend 27,000 feet.

Step three: Since Flowr is at 30 DME, add 30 DME + 81 NM = 111 DME to descend to 10,000 feet at Flowr intersection.

Step four: Add 5 NM + 111 DME = 116 DME to account for the slowdown from 300 KIAS during the descent to the crossing restriction of 250 KIAS at Flowr.

Step five: You will need to initiate the enroute descent at 116 DME from the BTG VOR. However, since you are on the LMT transition, you will not start using BTG DME until Moxee intersection which is defined as 96 DME from BTG. Therefore, you will need to start the descent 20 DME prior to Moxee, which is at 108 DME from LMT VOR (total distance from LMT to Moxee is 128 DME).

In addition, the interview questions that I know of factor a no-wind condition. However, as always, pay attention to the specifics of the interviewer's question. Never assume anything.

How to Figure Your Own VDP

Let's begin with a little background work on what the Visual Descent Point really is.

To begin with, here's what AIM paragraph 5-4-5.e. says:

Visual Descent Points (VDP) are incorporated in selected nonprecision approach procedures. The VDP is a defined point on the final approach course of a nonprecision straight-in approach procedure from which normal descent from the MDA to the runway touchdown point may be commenced, provided visual reference required by FAR Part 91.175(c)(3) is established. The VDP will normally be identified by DME on VOR and LOC procedures. The VDP is identified on the profile view of the approach chart by the symbol: V.

VDPs are intended to provide additional guidance where they are implemented. No special technique is required to fly a procedure with a VDP. The pilot should not descend below the MDA prior to reaching the VDP and acquiring the necessary visual reference.

Pilots not equipped to receive the VDP should fly the approach procedure as though no VDP had been provided.

Here are a few more points from TERPs that might help understand the utility of a VDP:

- A VDP will be for a normal descent to touchdown, usually a 3-degree glidepath;
- If a VASI is available on the runway, the VDP will align with the VASI glidepath.
- If a VASI is not available on the runway, the VDP will provide a normal glidepath to the runway threshold.

Please note that the AIM description of VDPs states that procedurally you **should not** descend below the MDA prior to the VDP, etc. However, in FAR Part 121.651(c)(4), there is implied approval to descend prior to the VDP if the descent from the MDA "to the runway cannot be made using normal procedures or rates of descent if descent is delayed until reaching that point."

In my opinion, every transport category aircraft I can think of should be able to comply with the intent of the VDP and not require an early descent even if we have the runway in sight. Besides, there may also be limiting obstacles to contend with, and a shallow glidepath or "dragged-in" glidepath can sometimes lead to visual illusions during the transition to landing.

Now that we've established some guidelines for using a VDP, what can you do in lieu of a VDP if there is not one published on the approach plate?

Some airline pilots are now using VDP-style techniques to build their own Planned Descent Point or PDP. This is simply a **tool** that enhances the normal transition to landing from the MDA, just like the VDP. Unlike the VDP, which has regulatory criteria to maintain from the TERPs handbook, a PDP is more like a pilot aid to use in the cockpit to help get the job done right. And, a PDP will never be published or have the regulatory backing of a VDP. However, it can really be a smart technique when a VDP is not otherwise available.

Here's the text version of a nonprecision approach plate that does not have a published VDP. Your goal is to calculate your own PDP. By the way, this technique of calculating a PDP works for any type of aircraft, regardless of speed flown on the approach.

The KGEG airport ILS Rwy 3 glideslope is NOTAMed out of service. Thus, you will need to fly the LOC (GS out) with MDA of 2760' (392'). There is a co-located DME with the ILS frequency. The FAF is identified by D6.1. The missed approach point is at the runway threshold identified by D1.6. In addition, with a ground speed of 120 knots, the timing on the approach is

2:15. If we assume that the ceiling and visibility is adequate to plan on seeing the runway environment from the MDA, what is your calculated PDP for the approach?

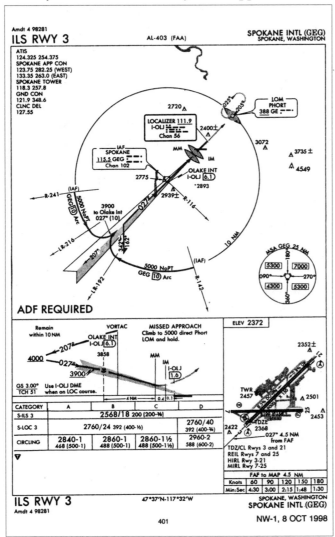

Illustration 4: ILS Rwy 3 Spokane Intl.

There are two methods to calculate a PDP. The most familiar method involves using DME. The other method involves the use of timing on the approach. Both methods work well for planning purposes. I'll summarize the differences in the methods after we solve the problem. Let's start with the DME method.

DME Method:

Step one, divide the HAT by 300. That would give us the distance in nautical miles that it would require to descend from the MDA to touchdown at the runway threshold with a 3° glidepath, or 300 feet per nautical mile. In our problem, $392/300 = 1.31$ NM. However, let's keep it simple and use $390/300 = 1.3$ NM.

Step two, determine the DME at the runway threshold. In our problem, the runway threshold is the same point as the missed approach point at 1.6 DME.

In those cases where the missed approach point is not identified by DME, yet it visually appears on the chart to be aligned with the runway threshold, and DME is used to identify the FAF, you should refer to the timing box for the approach plate to note the distance from the named FAF to the MAP. Then, subtract that distance in nautical miles from the FAF DME to get the DME at the threshold. This is always a good technique to use as a backup for your calculations because the small print on the approach plates does not always clearly portray distances on final approach.

Step three, add the two distances calculated from steps one and two above. This will give you an accurate DME for a PDP with a 3° glidepath to the runway threshold. In our problem, the PDP would be calculated to be at 2.91 DME, but our estimate of 2.9 DME is close enough for us to use.

Be extra cautious using this method when the DME to be used is from a VOR that is crossed earlier on the final approach; i.e., the DME may actually be getting larger the closer you get to touchdown. It may be helpful to sketch a layout of the runway versus DME source location to help clarify the math.

In fact, the Spokane ILS Rwy 3 portrays this situation. Notice that the GEG VORTAC is between the FAF and MAP.

Timing Method:

Step one, divide the HAT by 10. This gives us the time in seconds required to descend from the MDA to touchdown on the runway at 600 feet per minute rate of descent. In our problem, 392/10 = 39.2 seconds, but 39 seconds is close enough.

Step two, determine the timing required on the approach from the FAF to the MAP as shown in the timing box. It works for any chosen ground speed, but for our problem today at 120 knots GS, the timing is 2:15.

Step three, subtract the calculation in step one from the timing in step two. This gives us the timing from the FAF to the PDP. We always have the clock running from the time we cross the FAF anyway, so this requires no additional timing. In our problem, the timing for the PDP is at 2:15 - :39 = 1:36 on the approach.

So what's the difference between the two methods? The DME method uses 300 feet per nautical mile or a 3° glidepath to calculate the PDP. The timing method uses a constant 600 feet per minute rate of descent as the basis for calculating the PDP timing. In essence, the two methods may define a different point in space. However, at approximately 120 knots GS, the two different PDPs would be very close to each other.

Please bear in mind, also, that the formulas I've used here use some numbers that have been rounded off for ease of use. This also helps you do without a calculator.

Chapter 3

JUST ANOTHER APPROACH PLATE

Legends

A s I have helped prepare pilots for airline interviews, this has been one area where I encouraged self-study. It is an inefficient use of preparation time when it is just as easily studied at home, as the legend explanations are "self-explanatory." Remember, even an experienced pilot can learn something about approach plates!

You must know how to read *everything* on an approach chart and enroute chart. Jeppesen normally issues a small section of up to twenty pages which illustrates and defines all the lines, arrows, numbers, colors, symbols, shading, etc.

I would focus mainly on the approach chart legend followed by the enroute chart symbols and definitions of things such as MEA, MOCA, MRA, MCA, MAA, etc. Most of these items have dual references, one as illustrated on a sample chart plus another on a definition page.

Briefing Techniques

Assume that you are a Captain flying with a new First Officer, this is the first leg of the day, and you have never flown as a crew together. You have 60 seconds to brief your F/O on how you would like to fly an instrument approach procedure, with the weather forecast to be just above minimums.

What do you brief, and in what order? Jeppesen has reformatted many of their approach charts to allow a pilot to give a logically sequenced briefing simply by starting at the top left hand corner of these newly formatted approach plates and reading across and down-just like reading a book. It's a thing of beauty. Find a current Jeppesen approach chart to practice with.

However, for practice let's work with a
non-Jeppesen format to strengthen your technique.

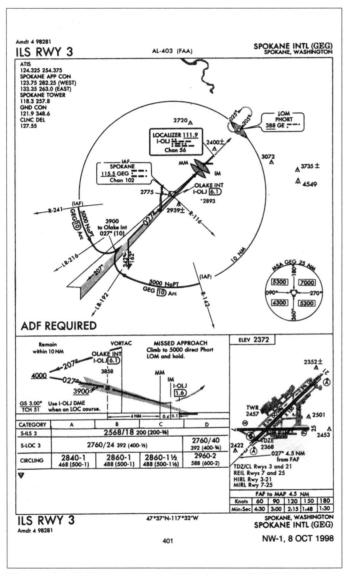

Illustration 5: Approach plate ILS Rwy 3 Spokane

Here's a condensed version of a crew's approach briefing, given the time constraints of an interview. If this question is asked and you are given a time frame in which to respond ("Please keep your briefing under one minute") you might leave out some of the detailed information on the chart that might have a lower priority.

1) Page number and date.

2) City name and approach name.

3) Minimum Safe Altitude (MSA), plus highest terrain depicted on approach chart.

4) Approach navaid frequency, ident, and course (include front course for a back course localizer).

5) Decision Altitude/Height (DA/H) or Minimum Descent Altitude (MDA). Use the approach category that you are given or use the one for your current aircraft and stick with it for the briefing.

6) Missed Approach Procedure, including holding pattern entry, if used.

7) Info from approach plan view; e.g., sequence of navaid tuning, cross-tuning of radials, DME sources, IAF, FAF, orientation of final course versus runway and airport, feeder fixes, NoPT, altitudes and restrictions.

8) Info from approach profile view; e.g., glide slope intercept altitude (GSIA), step-down fixes, altitude restrictions, timing and/or

DME to the missed approach point (M), visual descent point (VDP), or PDP if applicable.

9) Lighting systems; e.g., Visual Approach Slope Indicator (VASI) or Precision Approach Path Indicator (PAPI), type of approach light system (ALS).

10) Weather required, including visibility.

11) Backup approach type and minimums.

Here's a sample brief:

*"Let's fly the ILS Rwy 3 at Spokane, Washington on page 401, dated 8 Oct 98. The localizer identifier is **I-O-L-J** on frequency 111.9. The final approach course is 027 degrees. The glideslope crosses the outer marker at Olake at 3,858 feet. The decision altitude is 2,568 feet MSL, and the touchdown zone elevation is 2,368 feet MSL. The MSA is 7,000 feet to the northeast and 5,300 feet or lower everywhere else, with the highest terrain on the approach plate being to the right of our course about 15 miles from the airport. The missed approach is straight ahead to 5,000 feet to the Phort LOM and hold as depicted. It looks like a teardrop entry. The navaids will be set up progressively, using the GEG VOR DME (Chan 102) till ready to intercept final. Then we'll switch over to the IOLJ localizer DME of 111.9 (Chan 56). Published glideslope is 3,900 feet or*

lower if assigned. The missed approach point is at 1.6 DME off the localizer if we lose the glideslope, with a MDA of 2,760 feet. As a backup for the localizer, timing for the approach from Olake to the missed approach point is 2 minutes and 15 seconds. There is an ALSF-2 with VASI on Rwy 3. Any questions?"

Remember that this briefing will need to be short, even down to 60 seconds. If you do have more time, you might brief additional items such as the communication frequencies, glide slope angle, circling minimums, threshold crossing height (TCH), etc.

I realize that my 11-item list may seem too long to brief in one minute, but try it. I think you will find that with practice it can be done easily, smoothly, and confidently—even with an approach plate you've never seen before. Remember that your briefing needs to be accomplished in a professional manner in front of the interview board.

Final Approach Segment

So, what is the final approach segment? First of all, it really only applies to FAR Part 121 and 135 operators. Second, it is quite hard to find clear, complete, and distinct definitions in AIM and the FARs. Here's a question you might get:

At what point on an approach may you continue if the weather is reported below minimums?

The answer to this question comes from FAR Part 121.651(c) and 135.225(c) which are similar to each other.

121.651(c) If a pilot has begun the final approach segment of an instrument approach procedure in accordance with paragraph (b) of this section and after that receives a later weather report indicating below minimum conditions, the pilot may continue the approach to DA(H) or MDA.

Here is my version of the definition of "final approach segment" based on the combined definitions from the AIM glossary for "Final Approach Fix," "Final Approach Point (FAP)," and "Segments of an Instrument Approach Procedure." I'll try to keep it simple.

For a precision approach, such as an ILS, the final approach segment begins at the glide slope/path intercept point (GSIA), also shown as a lightning bolt on some approach plates. When Air Traffic Control (ATC) directs a lower-than-published glide slope/path intercept altitude, it is the resultant actual point of the glide slope/path intercept.

For a nonprecision approach, the final approach segment is designated by the Maltese Cross symbol, or final approach fix. With no depicted FAF (such as an on-airport VOR), the final approach segment where the aircraft is established inbound on the final approach course from the procedure turn and where the final approach descent may be commenced. This is also called the final approach point (FAP). The FAP serves as the FAF and identifies the beginning of the final approach segment.

In my experience, pilots will frequently mix terms and definitions of the FAF, FAP, and GSIA when determining the start of the final approach segment. Make sure you know the difference.

Approach Minimums

What is the weather required to fly a visual approach at an airport?

Answer: 1,000 foot ceiling and 3 statute miles visibility.

How far out from an airport can you accept clearance for a visual approach?

Answer: Any distance. [**Note:** there used to be a requirement to be no more than 35 NM from the airport, but that has been deleted from AIM. Some company OPSPECs still contain the 35 NM restriction] The pilot must, at all times, have either the airport or the preceding aircraft in sight.

What is the lowest visibility required for a Category I ILS?

Answer: 1,800 RVR. Refer to AIM Table 7-1-4.

You plan to fly the published ILS Rwy 23 at KLOW airport, but the glideslope is NOTAMed out of service. How does this impact your arrival planning?

Answer: You must now use the higher minimums for the LOC (GS out), thereby raising the MDA and visibility requirements.

Continued Descent Below DH/MDA

You are flying the ILS Rwy 23 at KLOW airport. At DH, all you can see is one sequenced flashing light. What do you do?

Answer: Refer to FAR Part 91.175(c) for the whole answer but here we will focus on one specific and little used element of the requirements to descend below the DH.

Specifically, if the approach light system is distinctly visible and identifiable to the pilot, the pilot may continue to descend no lower than 100 feet above the touchdown zone elevation using the approach lights as a reference unless the red terminating bars or the red side row bars are also distinctly visible and identifiable. If they are, the pilot may continue to descend to land.

In addition, if at any time another element of the "runway environment" as listed in 91.175 comes into view, the pilot may also continue to descend to land.

Where's the Missed Approach Point?

For a nonprecision approach, the missed approach point (MAP) is usually visually identified by a capitalized and bold "**M**" in the Jeppesen approach plates, or at the end of the solid line of the profile view for NOS plates (National Ocean Services). In many cases, the missed approach point is closely aligned with the end of the runway threshold.

There are several ways to identify the missed approach point:

1) Published DME at the MAP.

2) Navaid such as a middle marker (MM).

3) Timing from the FAF.

As a backup, to determine the distance from the FAF to the MAP (which is usually the runway threshold) always refer to the timing chart near the bottom of the approach plate. One of the three lines in the chart will always provide the nautical miles from the FAF to the MAP.

For a precision approach like the ILS, the MAP is that point at which the aircraft reaches the DA(H).

Circling Approaches

*If visual reference is lost while circling to
land from an instrument approach, what
action should the pilot take?*

Answer: Refer to AIM 5-4-18. If visual
reference is lost while circling to land from an
instrument approach, the missed approach specified
for that particular procedure must be followed
(unless an alternate missed approach procedure is
specified by ATC). To become established on the
prescribed missed approach course, the pilot should
make an initial climbing turn toward the landing
runway and continue the turn until established on
the missed approach course. Inasmuch as the
circling maneuver may be accomplished in more
than one direction, different patterns will be
required to become established on the prescribed
missed approach course, depending on the aircraft
position at the time visual reference is lost.

To be clear, the missed approach procedure
to be flown will be that procedure described for the
approach that was flown to a particular runway.
Initially, however, the pilot must turn toward the
landing runway which he was circling to land on.
Then he will intercept the missed approach
procedure for the approach that was flown. The
priority here is to ensure that the airplane remains

within the obstacle clearance areas while maneuvering for the landing/missed approach.

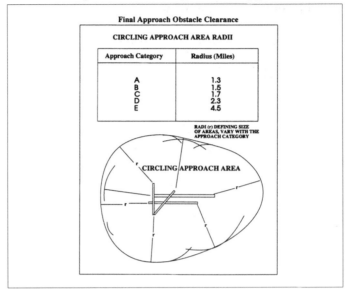

Illustration 6: Circling Approach Area

Illustration 6 depicts the obstacle clearance dimensions within the circling approach area.

AIM uses diagram 5-4-8 to illustrate the missed approach procedure if visual reference is lost during the circling maneuver.

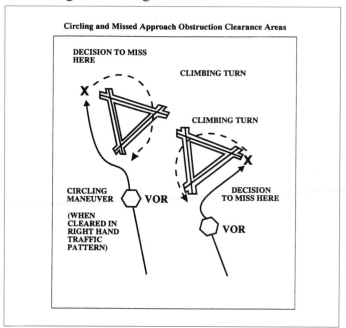

Illustration 7: Circling and Missed Approach Maneuvers

NOTES

Chapter 4

UNDERSTANDING AIM

Which minimum IFR altitudes include obstacle clearance of 1,000 feet in nonmountainous terrain and 2,000 feet in designated mountainous terrain?

Min IFR Altitude	1,000 ft.	2,000 ft./Mtns
MEA	Yes	Yes
MOCA	Yes	Yes
MSA-Sector	Yes	No
MSA-Emergency	Yes	Yes
MVA	Yes	Yes

Airport Lighting Aids and Markings

*Define Pilot Controlled Airport Lighting
and describe how to use it if the tower or
FSS is closed.*

Answer: Refer to AIM 2-1-7. Pilot Control
of Airport Lighting. Public use airports have
information in the Airport/Facility Directory or
approach plate/airport diagram that identifies the
lighting system, runway that it's installed on, and
the frequency that is used to activate the system.

The lighting may be any of a number of
combinations of approach lights, runway lights,
taxiway lights, or VASI that are radio controlled by
the pilot. The control system responds to a series of
7, 5, or 3 microphone clicks within 5 seconds to
illuminate the airport lights during night conditions
when the tower or FSS is closed. The lights are then
illuminated for 15 minutes. The number of clicks
determines the intensity level of the lighting, with 7
clicks recommended to be used first to turn the
lights on at the highest intensity. 5 and 3 clicks are
normally for medium and low intensity lighting.

*Describe what Touchdown Zone Lighting
(TDZL) looks like.*

Answer: Refer to AIM 2-1-4. Runway Edge
Light Systems. Touchdown zone lighting consists
of two rows of transverse white light bars disposed
symmetrically about the runway centerline in the
runway touchdown zone. The system starts 100 feet
from the landing threshold and extends to 3,000 feet

from the threshold or the midpoint of the runway, whichever is the lesser.

Describe what type of distance remaining indications there are on a precision approach runway.

?

Answer: Refer to AIM 2-1-4, 2-1-5, and 2-3-13. There is a change in the runway lighting the last 3,000 feet of the runway. In addition to the runway distance remaining signs on the side of the runway every 1,000 feet, starting at:

1) 3,000 feet remaining, the white runway centerline lights begin to alternate with the red for the next 2,000 feet;

2) 2,000 feet remaining, the runway edge lights change from white to yellow for the rest of the runway;

3) 1,000 feet remaining, the runway centerline lights change to all red.

Define and describe High Intensity Runway Lighting (HIRL).

Answer: Refer to AIM 2-1-4. Runway edge lights outline the edges of runways during periods of darkness or restricted visibility conditions. These light systems are classified according to the intensity or brightness they are capable of producing. In this case, HIRL is High Intensity Runway Lighting. Others are Medium (MIRL) and Low (LIRL) Intensity Lighting.

The runway edge lights are white, except on instrument runways where yellow replaces white for the last 2,000 feet, or half the runway length, whichever is less, to form a caution zone for landing.

The lights marking the ends of the runway emit red light toward the runway to indicate the end of runway to a departing aircraft and emit green outward from the runway end to indicate the threshold to landing aircraft.

After landing and exiting the runway, how do you know when you are clear of the runway?

Answer: Refer to AIM 2-3-5. An aircraft exiting a runway is not clear of the runway until all parts of the aircraft have crossed the applicable holding position markings.

That's great, but can you describe or diagram the holding position markings? Many pilots can't. It's another one of those things you see and comply with so often that you take it for granted. Perhaps this analogy will help etch the markings in your memory.

As you are driving down a two-lane highway, you notice that there is a series of yellow markings in two rows dividing the roadway into two lanes. Of course, we know that if the solid (continuous) yellow line is on our side of the highway, with the dashed yellow line on the other side of the highway, this indicates that we cannot pass another vehicle or cross the solid yellow line.

Conversely, if the dashed yellow line is on our side of the highway, with the solid yellow line on the other side, we are permitted to pass another vehicle or cross the dashed line.

We can use this analogy to exiting a runway. But, first, let's look at these runway holding position markings.

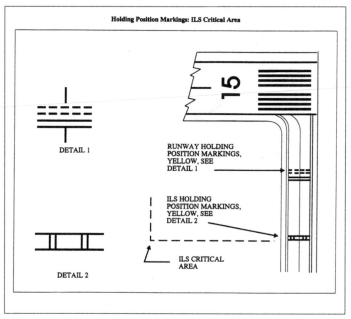

Illustration 8: Runway Holding

Notice here that the dashed yellow lines are on the runway side and the solid yellow lines are on the taxiway side.

Here's how the analogy fits. In the same fashion that when on the highway with the solid yellow line on your side, that precludes you from crossing the yellow line, the same would apply as you are taxiing out to a runway. You are automatically expected to not cross the yellow lines of the runway holding position markings unless you have additional and specific clearance from ATC. Likewise, when exiting the runway, there is implied permission to cross the dashed yellow lines that you first encounter, just as on a highway.

Entering the Holding Pattern

Here's a subject where it is easy for the sun to either shine or slip behind a fog bank. Here are a few questions we know are being asked that I'm certain will help simplify your study of holding patterns.

How soon before an assigned holding fix should you begin to slow to holding speed?

Answer: Refer to AIM 5-3-7.d. When an aircraft is three minutes or less from a clearance limit and a clearance beyond the fix has not been received, the pilot is expected to start a speed reduction so that the aircraft will cross the fix at or below the maximum holding airspeed.

"You are cleared to hold southeast of the RCK VOR 120 degree radial at the 20

DME fix at 9000 feet, standard pattern."
Diagram the holding pattern.

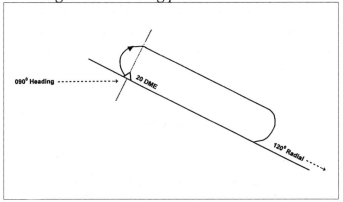

Illustration 9: Holding Pattern

What are the maximum holding airspeeds
and timing for the inbound leg?

Answer: Refer to AIM 5-3-7.j.2. AIM recently published a change to the holding airspeeds. It's a lot simpler now, but, of course, involves a big change for all of us to memorize. The military aircraft specifics are now generalized into USAF and Navy. Maximum timing for the inbound leg is 1 minute at 14,000 feet and below, 1.5 minutes above 14,000 feet. All aircraft will comply with the following maximum speeds:

Altitude (MSL)	Airspeed (KIAS)
MHA - 6,000'	200
6,001' - 14,000'	230
14,001' and above	265

The following are exceptions to the maximum holding airspeeds:

1) From 6,001' to 14,000' may be restricted to 210 KIAS.

2) All altitudes may be restricted to 175 KIAS.

3) At USAF airfields only, a maximum of 310 KIAS.

4) At Navy airfields only, a maximum of 230 KIAS.

In the above holding pattern clearance, assume that we are arriving from the west on a heading of 090 degrees as we cross the holding fix at 20 DME. What type of holding pattern entry should we use?

Answer. Refer to AIM 5-3-7.

STANDARD PATTERN

Illustration 10: Holding Pattern Entry Procedures

In our scenario, our aircraft would be coming in from sector (b) on a heading of 090°. Therefore, the recommended pattern entry is a teardrop entry. AIM recommends the following type entries based on the arrival sectors as labeled above. Refer to AIM 5-3-7 for detailed descriptions of these procedures.

- Sector (a) Parallel procedure.
- Sector (b) Teardrop procedure.
- Sector (c) Direct entry procedure.

In my experience with interviewing pilots, rather than fumble through a lot of memory gimmicks or formulas or hand gymnastics, the best approach seems to come simply with drawing the holding pattern as we did above, then also drawing a line showing the path of entry at the holding fix. From there it seems to be quite easy for most pilots, because the three types of entry can be pretty obvious once you visualize the arrival.

Two helpful hints. First, remember how the holding pattern entry circle looks, especially how the 70 degree sector is aligned. Second, remember that AIM reminds us that these entry procedures are **recommended** by the FAA. They are not mandatory and can be modified as long as you stay within the protected airspace, and, of course, advise ATC before deviating from these recommended procedures.

In the above holding pattern clearance, assume there is a crosswind from the southwest that requires a 10 degree crab into the wind (left heading correction) on the inbound leg, or a heading of 290 degrees. What is the recommended technique for correcting for winds on the outbound leg?

Answer: Refer to AIM 5-3-7. When outbound, triple the inbound drift correction to avoid major turning adjustments. In this problem, on the outbound leg you should use a crab angle of 30 degrees into the wind (right heading correction), or a heading of 150 degrees.

Airspace and Operations

What is Class B airspace?

Answer: Refer to AIM 3-2-3. Generally, it is that airspace from the surface to 10,000 feet MSL surrounding the nation's busiest airports. Some Class B airspace areas resemble upside-down wedding cakes. An ATC clearance is required for all aircraft to operate in the area.

Also refer to FAR Part 91.117(c). Maximum airspeed in the airspace underlying a Class B airspace area is 200 KIAS. There is no specific

speed restriction within Class B airspace except for
the 250 KIAS limit when below 10,000 feet MSL.

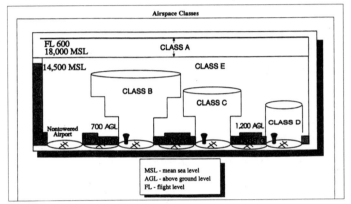

Illustration 11: Airspace Classes

When given a clearance to taxi to a
runway, what runways or taxiways may be
crossed?

Answer: Refer to AIM 4-3-18. When ATC
authorizes an aircraft to "taxi to" an assigned
takeoff runway, the absence of holding instructions
authorizes the aircraft to "cross" all runways which
the taxi route intersects except the assigned takeoff
runway. It does not include authorization to "taxi
onto" or "cross" the assigned takeoff runway at any
point. In order to preclude misunderstandings in
radio communications, ATC will not use the word
"cleared" in conjunction with authorization for
aircraft to taxi.

Wake Turbulence

Wake turbulence is a topic under the
heading of "Safety of Flight" that deserves your full

attention. As such, please take a few minutes to study the characteristics, behavior, and recommended avoidance procedures from AIM Chapter 7, Section 3. My experience is that more airlines are using this as a subject question for the technical interviews.

?
Which flight conditions create the most severe flight hazard by generating wingtip vortices of the greatest strength?

Answer: Refer to AIM 7-3-3. The greatest vortex strength occurs when the generating aircraft is HEAVY, CLEAN, and SLOW.

?
What effect would a light crosswind have on the wingtip vortices generated by a large airplane that has just taken off?

Answer: Refer to AIM 7-3-4. A crosswind will decrease the lateral movement of the upwind vortex and increase the movement of the downwind vortex. Thus a light wind with a cross runway component of 1 to 5 knots could result in the upwind vortex remaining in the touchdown zone for

a period of time and hasten the drift of the
downwind vortex toward another runway.

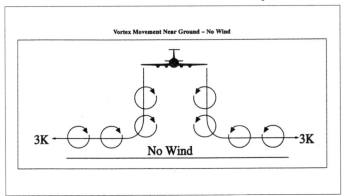

Illustration 12: Vortex Movement Near Ground

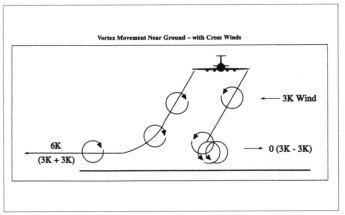

**Illustration 13: Vortex Movement Near Ground with
Crosswind**

*What wind condition prolongs the hazards
of wake turbulence on a landing runway
for the longest period of time?*

Answer: Refer to AIM 7-3-4. The light
quartering tailwind requires maximum caution
because a tailwind condition can move the vortices

of the preceding aircraft forward into the touchdown zone.

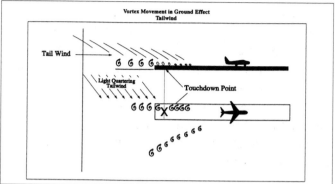

Illustration 14: Vortex Movement in Ground Effect/Tailwind

What wake turbulence separation is required for small aircraft following bigger airplanes on landing approach?

Answer: Refer to AIM 7-3-9. ATC separation minimums for wake turbulence during the landing approach are provided for small aircraft:

Small behind large aircraft	4 miles
Small behind B757 aircraft	5 miles
Small behind heavy jet	6 miles

One erroneous, yet common, answer that I hear from pilots is that they need two or three minutes behind other aircraft on final approach. **No!** The only place that you can effectively use timing for spacing is when you are sitting number one for takeoff behind another aircraft that is already on the takeoff roll. There is no way that you can accurately "hack your clock" airborne to determine when the aircraft in front of you is passing over a particular landmark—you would be guessing as much as anything. Alas, ATC must provide you with speed restrictions and distance information to comply with wake turbulence separation standards when airborne. Note: TCAS is also a great airborne tool for determining your own separation. However, ATC is still responsible for separation as it is explained in AIM. Perhaps pilots will have more individual capability and responsibility as TCAS becomes more widely used.

Please note that this section of AIM seems particularly confusing because there are several different phases of flight that are addressed in different paragraphs; i.e., cruise, takeoff, and landing. In addition, it is common for individual air carriers and the military to have minor differences from AIM. My recommendation is to answer the question with the criteria provided by your own company OPSPECS or flight rules if they are different from AIM.

This is also a good place to take note of the basic definitions of small, large, and heavy aircraft. These are provided in the glossary section at the end of the study guide.

NOTES

Chapter 5

DEFINING THE FARS

Instrument Flight Rules - FARs

What are the requirements to continue descent below the Decision Height or Minimum Descent Altitude?

?

Answer: Refer to FAR 91.175(c). Three requirements must be met:

1) The aircraft is in a position to make a normal descent to touchdown within the touchdown zone.

2) The flight visibility is not less than required by the approach.

3) At least one of the following visual references is distinctly visible and identifiable to the pilot:

The ALS, except that the pilot may not descend below 100 feet above the TDZE using the approach lights as a reference unless the red terminating bars or the red side row bars are also distinctly visible and identifiable.

The threshold, threshold markings, or threshold lights.

The runway end identifier lights (REIL).

The visual approach slope indicator (VASI).

The touchdown zone, touchdown zone markings, or touchdown zone lights.

The runway, runway markings, or runway lights.

?

After what point may you continue an approach if the weather goes below minimums?

Answer: Refer to FAR 121.651(c) and 135.225(c). The criteria are identical for airline and charter operations. These regulations state that, "If a pilot has begun the final approach segment of an instrument approach procedure in accordance with paragraph (b) of this section and after that receives a later weather report indicating below-minimum conditions, the pilot may continue the approach to DH or MDA."

Specifically, if flying an ILS, you may continue the approach after you have already intercepted the glideslope at or below the published glideslope intercept altitude..

On a non-precision approach, you may continue once inside the FAF.

What radio calls are required under IFR in a radar environment?

?

Answer: Refer to FAR 91.183, 91.187, and AIM 4-4-3, AIM 4-4-6.

1) Time and altitude at each designated reporting point. When in radar contact, only those requested by ATC.

2) Any unforecast weather.

3) Any information regarding safety of flight.

4) Any malfunction of navigational, approach, or communication equipment.

5) For holding, the time and altitude reaching and leaving the clearance limit.

6) Read back altitudes, altitude restrictions, and vectors (headings).

What is the requirement for VOR checks for IFR operations?

?

Answer: Refer to FAR 91.171. No person may operate a civil aircraft under IFR using the VOR for navigation unless the VOR:

1) Has been operationally checked within the preceding 30 days, and

2) With ground VOT/VOR checkpoint accuracy of +/- 4 degrees, or

3) With airborne checkpoint accuracy of +/- 6 degrees, or

4) With dual system VOR accuracy of +/- 4 degrees of each other.

 What is the lost communication procedure when in IFR conditions?

   Answer: Refer to FAR 91.185 and AIM 6-4-1. The procedure involves three elements: route, altitude, and clearance limit. In each case, the pilot shall continue the flight according to the following priorities:

Route.
   1) By the route assigned in the last ATC clearance received.

   2) If being radar vectored, by the direct route from the point of radio failure to the fix, route, or airway specified in the vector clearance.

   3) In the absence of an assigned route, by the route that ATC has advised may be expected in a further clearance, or

   4) In the absence of an assigned route or a route that ATC has advised may be expected in a further clearance by the route filed in the flight plan.

Altitude.

At the HIGHEST of the following **for the route segment being flown:**

1) The altitude or flight level assigned in the last ATC clearance received.

2) The MEA.

3) The altitude or flight level ATC has advised may be expected in a further clearance.

Leave clearance limit.

1) When the clearance limit is a fix from which an approach begins, commence descent or descent and approach as close as possible to the expect further clearance time if one has been received, or if one has not been received, as close as possible to the ETA as calculated from the filed or amended ETA.

2) If the clearance limit is not a fix from which an approach begins, leave the clearance limit at the expect further clearance time if one has been received, or if none has been received, upon arrival over the clearance limit, and proceed to a fix from which an approach begins and commence descent or descent and approach as close as possible to the ETA as calculated from the filed or amended ETE.

When do you need an alternate for your destination?

Answer: Refer to FAR 91.167 and FAR 121.619 (Domestic operations). Using the **1-2-3** rule: an alternate is not required if the weather is equal to or better than:

1) plus or minus 1 hour of the ETA

2) 2,000 foot ceiling

3) 3 statute miles visibility

Refer to FAR 121.621 (flag operations). An alternate is not required if:

1) the flight is scheduled for not more than 6 hours, and

2) plus or minus 1 hour of the ETA the ceiling will be

a. at least 1,500 feet above the lowest circling MDA, if a circling approach is required and authorized; or

b. at least 1,500 feet above the lowest published instrument approach minimum or 2,000 feet above the airport elevation, whichever is greater; and

c. the visibility at that airport will be at least 3 miles, or 2 miles more than the lowest applicable visibility minimums, whichever is greater.

*When do you need an alternate for a
departure airport for airline operations?*

Answer: Refer to FAR 121.617. If the
weather conditions at the takeoff airport are below
the landing minimums in the certificate holder's
operations specifications for that airport, an
alternate airport that meets alternate airport weather
requirements must be designated for the flight. For
two engine aircraft, the alternate must be within one
hour from the departure airport at normal cruising
speed in still air with one engine inoperative. For
three or four engine aircraft, the alternate must be
within two hours.

*What are the alternate airport weather
minimums for airline operations?*

Answer: Refer to FAR 121.625. Alternate
airport weather must meet the minimums specified
in the operator's operations specifications.

However, referencing FAR 91.169(c), the
basic requirements for weather at an alternate are
600/2 for a precision approach or 800/2 for a
nonprecision approach. To be safe, refer to the back
of the airport diagram page to determine alternate
weather required for that specific airport. Company
OPSPECs may authorize lower or different
minimums.

In a turbine powered airplane with a pressurized cabin, when are the pilots required to wear an oxygen mask?

Answer: Refer to FAR 121.333. Above FL 410, at least one pilot at the flight controls is required to don and use his mask. Above FL 250, if one pilot leaves his seat, the remaining pilot shall don and use his mask until the other pilot returns.

What are the visibility minimums for takeoff from a civil airport?

Answer: Refer to FAR 91.175 (f). For operations under FAR 121 or 135, the OPSPECS dictate minimum visibility requirements. If no takeoff minimums are prescribed for a particular airport, the following minimums apply:

1) Aircraft with two engines or less, 1 statute mile visibility.

2) Aircraft having more than two engines, 1/2 statute mile visibility.

For airline operations it is common to refer to the back of the airport diagram page to determine the visibility required for takeoff on specific runways. Differences from one runway to another may stem from differing lighting capabilities. OPSPECs authorize operations in one of the three categories you will see on the following takeoff visibility table: standard as described above, adequate visual reference capability to 1600 RVR or 1/4 statute mile, or with CL & RCLM to as low as 600 RVR for the TDZ, Mid, and Rollout. Here's how that table might look:

Rwys 23R, 05L

	CL & RCLM	Adeq Vis Ref	STD
1 & 2 Eng	TDZ RVR 6 Mid RVR 6 Rollout RVR 6	RVR 16 or 1/4	RVR 50 or 1
3 & 4 Eng	TDZ RVR 6 Mid RVR 6 Rollout RVR 6	RVR 16 or 1/4	RVR 24 or 1/2

For interview purposes, **unless told otherwise**, I believe it is safe to assume that you could use the lowest category, 600 RVR. Remember, at these low visibilities, a takeoff alternate may be required.

NOTES

Chapter 6

IF YOU DON'T LIKE THE WEATHER . . .

Reading a METAR and TAF

Get very comfortable with the reading of a TAF and METAR. Airline expectations of you are that if you are a competent pilot you should certainly know how to read a weather report accurately.

The Department of Transportation and the Federal Aviation Administration published a great handout entitled "New Aviation Weather Formats: METAR/TAF." It's available free of charge at FSDOs or by calling the FAA Office of Assistant Administrator for System Safety in Washington,

D.C. (202/267-7770) and asking for publication number FAA/ASY-20 96/001.

Also, refer to AIM 7-1-10 for a decoding key for the ASOS (METAR) observations. AIM 7-1-27 contains a complete key for METAR and TAF formats.

Here's a couple of notes that will help as you study and learn the formats. First, when METAR data is missing from the body of the report (e.g., dew point), it is simply omitted and the user must know the sequence to recognize this. Some exceptions apply in the remarks section such as RVRNO or SLPNO when RVR or SLP are normally reported but not currently available.

Second, to help remember the sequence, think of the **3W's** at the beginning — **Where, When,** and **Wind**. This works equally well for METAR as well as TAF. Here's a sample METAR format and explanation:

METAR KDEN 081954Z AUTO 32015G23KT 1/2SM R34R/2600FT TSRA OVC012CB 14/11 A2997 RMK AO2 SLP149 T01410113

1) Where: **KDEN** is the four letter ICAO station identifier for Denver.

2) When: the **8**th day of the month at **1954** Zulu time.

3) **AUTO** is included only at a fully automated ASOS/AWOS site without human intervention.

4) Wind: **320** true direction to the nearest 10 degrees. When wind direction varies 60 degrees or more and wind is greater than 6 knots, a **V** will be placed between the two 3 digit numbers representing the variance in wind direction. Velocity is **15 gusting to 23 knots. VRB** is used when wind direction is variable and speed is less than or equal to 6 knots.

5) Visibility: **1/2** statute miles visibility. Also reported in miles and fractions. **R34R/2600FT** means runway visual range for runway **34R is 2600** feet. May also use a **V** if the RVR is variable between two 4-digit values.

6) Significant Present Weather: **TSRA** means a thunderstorm with moderate rain. The format is a two character descriptor sometimes followed by a two character weather phenomenon. Please refer to AIM or the FAA METAR handout to decipher the many combinations of weather. A short review prior to the technical interview may be necessary, although many abbreviations make sense with experience and study.

7) Clouds: Specifies the cloud amount, height in hundreds of feet, and type. **OVC012CB** means that overcast clouds are present at 1200 feet consisting of cumulonimbus (**CB**)clouds. Cloud amounts are classified into the following five categories:

SKC: Sky Clear

FEW: 0 - 2 eights coverage of sky

SCT: 3 - 4 eights coverage of sky

BKN: 5 - 7 eights coverage of sky

OVC: 8 eights coverage of sky

8) Temperature/Dew Point: Listed in degrees Celsius. When temperatures are below zero degrees Celsius, they are preceded by "**M**" for **Minus**. In our example, temperature is 14 degrees Celsius, dew point is 11 degrees Celsius.

9) Altimeter Setting: "**A**" indicates setting in inches of mercury for the U.S. Consists of 4 digits, inches and hundredths, just like we read from ATC and set in our altimeter. In our example, 29.97 inches.

10) Remarks: **RMK** in the example

AO1/AO2: Classification of the ASOS/AWOS site used for the automatic reporting. **A02** means an automated observation with precipitation discriminator (rain/snow).

SLP: Sea Level Pressure reported as the last three digits in millibars (hectoPascals) to the nearest tenth. This should match up with the altimeter setting as described above. In our example, **149** means 1014.9 millibars, which can also be set in many airplane altimeters alongside the inches of mercury.

A technique I use to ensure proper conversion is to remember that I will need to place the number "10" or "9" in front of the 3 digits in the METAR. I chose the prefix that gives me the closest answer to "1000.0"

If the METAR showed SLP884, this would necessitate using a "9" in front to give me 988.4 millibars as the proper answer. If I had used a "10", 1088.4 millibars is way off target and not realistic.

T: this 9 character code breaks down the temperature and dew point to the nearest tenth of a degree Celsius. In our example, **T01410113**, "**T**" stands for temperature, "**0**" as the next digit indicates a positive temperature ("**1**" is used to indicate a negative temperature), "**141**" indicates the temperature as 14.1 degrees Celsius; similarly, the "**0113**" indicates the dewpoint as a positive 11.3 degrees Celsius.

What defines a ceiling?

Answer: Refer to AIM Glossary. The heights above the earth's surface of the lowest layer of clouds or obscuring phenomena that is reported as "broken," "overcast," or "obscuration," and not classified as "thin" or "partial."

In our example, **OVC012CB** defines an overcast ceiling of 1200 feet above the surface, or AGL.

Fog Formation

What are the three types of fog and their differences?

Refer to *Aviation Weather*, AC 00-6A, Chapter 12.

Answer:

1)   Upslope fog

2)   Advection fog

3)   Radiation fog

First, the similarities are that all three involve **stable moist air** that has been **cooled** to its **dewpoint**. Next, here are the differences:

Fog Type	Cause	Winds	Skies	Density
Upslope	Air moves up sloping terrain	Light to Moderate	Clear or Cloudy	Dense
Advection	Air moves over colder surface	Up to 15 knots	Clear or Cloudy	Dense
Radiation	Ground radiates heat and cools, and also cools air above it	Calm	Clear	Shallow

Thunderstorms

What are the three elements required for the development of a thunderstorm?

Answer:

1) Sufficient water vapor,

2) An unstable lapse rate,

3) An initial upward boost (lifting) to start the storm process in motion.

Refer to *Aviation Weather*, AC 00-6A, Chapter 11.

What are the three stages and characteristics of a thunderstorm?

Answer:Refer to *Aviation Weather*, AC 00-6A, Chapter 11.

Stage	Vertical	Rain
Cumulus	Updraft 3,000 fpm	Small drops growing to large in updraft
Mature	Downdraft 2,500 fpm plus updrafts 6,000 fpm	Heavy raindrops and cold downdrafts
Dissipating	Downdrafts only	Rain ending

You are cruising at high altitude on a course of 020 degrees with isolated thunderstorms in the area approaching your altitude. You see a thunderstorm in the cumulus stage at your 12 o'clock

*position, and the cruise winds are 290/75.
Which way should you deviate around the
storm?*

Answer: Refer to AIM 7-1-26 and *Aviation Weather*, AC 00-6A, Chapter 11. Based upon my own experience and common practice, when given a choice, always deviate upwind, or, to the left in this example, to avoid the blowoff effects of the thunderstorm. In addition, if it is necessary to overfly the cumulus, maintain at least 2,000 feet vertical separation from the storm.

AIM and *Aviation Weather* both recommend circumnavigating the storm by at least 20 miles and to clear the top of a known or suspected severe thunderstorm by at least 1,000 feet altitude for each 10 knots of wind speed at the cloud top. This should exceed the altitude capability of most aircraft.

Windshear

?

What are the characteristics of windshear?

Answer: Windshear is defined in the AIM glossary as a change in wind speed and/or wind direction in a short distance resulting in a tearing or shearing effect. It can exist in a horizontal or vertical direction and occasionally in both.

Severe wind shear is defined as any rapid change in wind direction or velocity which causes airspeed changes greater than 15 knots or vertical speed changes greater than 500 feet per minute.

Many airlines have included additional criteria to define severe windshear such as an unusual throttle position over a significant amount of time, a pitch change of more than 5 degrees, or a glideslope deviation of more than 1 dot. (Hint: To help me visualize these criteria, I think of my aircraft as coupled to the autopilot and autothrottles while flying a normal ILS approach. This allows me to sit back and monitor the autopilot and autothrottle compensation for the windshear while trying to maintain glidepath.)

What are the common sources or generators of wind shear conditions?

Answer: Refer to *Aviation Weather*, AC 00-6A, Chapter 9. Thunderstorms, temperature inversions, and jet stream winds are the common sources.

What are the characteristics of a microburst?

Answer: The AIM glossary defines a microburst as a small downburst with outbursts of damaging winds extending 2.5 miles or less. In spite of its small horizontal scale, an intense microburst could induce wind speeds as high as 150 knots. Its characteristics also include:

Size — 1 mile in diameter below the clouds to 2.5 miles as it expands or "mushrooms" just above the ground.

Intensity — Downdrafts can be as strong as 6,000 feet per minute. Horizontal winds near the ground can be as strong as 45 knots resulting in a 90 knot wind shear effect.

Visual signs — Heavy rain shaft below a thunderstorm, light rain with virga or a ring of blowing dust.

Duration — An individual microburst will seldom last longer than 15 minutes. The horizontal winds increase the most during the first five minutes, with the peak winds lasting two to four minutes.

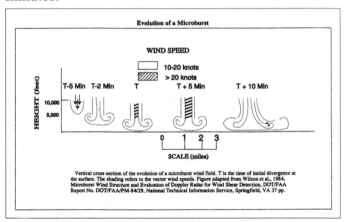

Illustration 15: Evolution of a Microburst

What is your windshear recovery procedure?

Answer: Refer to your airplane flight manual or company OPSPECs for guidance. Typical windshear recovery procedures for the airlines include:

- Select maximum thrust
- Rotate to 15 degrees pitch or the stall limit, whichever is less

- Do not change configuration
- Notify ATC

For the interview as well as for your day-to-day flying, it's critical that you know how to recognize and recover from a severe windshear encounter in your aircraft. Know your procedures well enough that you can be confident and respond to the question without hesitation or second-guessing.

Miscellaneous Weather Phenomena

Describe mountain waves and standing lenticular clouds.

Answer: Refer to *Aviation Weather*, AC 00-6A, Chapter 7 and 9 and AIM 7-5-5.

Mountain waves occur when air is being blown over a mountain range or even the ridge of a sharp bluff area. As the air hits the upwind side of the range, it starts to climb, thus creating what is generally a smooth updraft which turns into a turbulent downdraft as the air passes the crest of the ridge. From this point, for many miles downwind, there will be a series of downdrafts and updrafts. All it takes to form a mountain wave is wind blowing across the range at 15 knots or better at an intersection angle of not less than 30 degrees.

Standing lenticular altocumulus clouds, characterized by smooth, polished edges, are formed on the crests of waves created by mountains waves with sufficient moisture present. Satellite photos of the Rockies have shown clouds associated with mountain waves extending as far as 700 miles downwind of the range. As the moist air rises and cools to its dewpoint, this lens-shaped cloud forms. As the air then descends and warms, the cloud dissipates. These clouds show little movement, hence the name "standing." Winds blowing through such clouds, however, can be quite strong. The presence of these clouds is a good indication of very strong turbulence and they should be avoided.

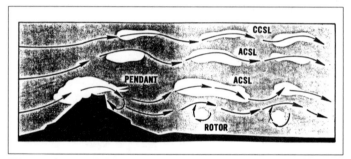

Illustration 16, Mountain Wave

Describe localized wind effects such as those given the names "Chinook" or "Santa Ana."

Answer: Refer to *Aviation Weather*, AC 00-6A, Chapter 4.

These are mountain winds, or katabatic winds that originate because cold, heavy air spills down sloping terrain displacing warmer, less dense air ahead of it. Air is heated and dried as it flows down slope, and sometimes the descending air becomes warmer than the air it replaces.

Many katabatic winds recurring in local areas have been given colorful names to highlight their dramatic, local effect.

The "Chinook" is a katabatic downslope wind. Air cools as it moves upslope and warms as it blows downslope. It occasionally produces dramatic warming over the plains just east of the Rocky Mountains.

Similarly, the "Santa Ana" winds are warm winds descending from the Sierras into the Santa Ana valley of California.

Describe the differences between a warm front, cold front, and stationary front.

Answer: Refer to *Aviation Weather*, AC 00-6A, Chapter 8.

Cold fronts tend to be faster moving than warm fronts, with an increase in pressure. Defined as colder surface air overtaking and replacing warmer air, a fast moving cold front produces showers and thunderstorms. A slower moving cold front contains embedded CBs and thunderstorms.

A warm front tends to move about half the speed of a cold front but with comparable winds and is marked by a decrease in pressure. Defined as advancing warmer air replacing colder air, warm front clouds are stratiform and widespread with continuous precipitation.

A stationary front results when neither air mass replaces the other. It has little or no movement and winds are nearly parallel to the front.

 What are the weather characteristics usually associated with an unstable air mass and a stable air mass?

Answer: Refer to *Aviation Weather*, AC 00-6A, Chapter 8.

Unstable Air	Stable Air
Cumuloform clouds	Stratiform clouds and fog
Showery precipitation	Continuous precipitation
Rough air/turbulence	Smooth air
Good visibility, except in blowing obstructions	Fair to poor visibility in haze and smoke

 How does your wind drift angle change at cruise altitude as you cross frontal boundaries?

Answer: In the northern hemisphere, after passing through the front, you will notice more wind from the right (or, less wind component from the left) causing a drift angle more to the left. This effect is due to the characteristics of frontal formation and does not depend upon the direction from which you approach the front.

 What types of turbulence can you encounter in an airplane?

Answer: Refer to *Aviation Weather*, AC 00-6A, Chapter 9. **Clear air turbulence (CAT) in**

the vicinity of the jet stream; **wake turbulence** behind other aircraft; **convective turbulence** in the areas of thunderstorm activity to include a gust front; and **mechanical turbulence** near the surface around large structures that interfere with airflow and around mountain waves at altitude.

What is virga?

?

Answer: Refer to *Aviation Weather*, AC 00-6A, Chapter 5. Water or ice particles falling from a cloud, usually looking like wisps or streaks, and evaporating before reaching the ground.

NOTES

Chapter 7

USING YOUR HANDS TO FLY

The emphasis in this chapter will be in two major areas:

1) knowledge and descriptions of the aircraft that you currently fly; and

2) general knowledge about aircraft, some of which is derived from the ATP and FEX written test guides.

Since it would be overly presumptuous and improperly omniscient for me to dedicate this book to the systems descriptions of all the aircraft that pilot interview candidates have flown, please allow me to generalize and list areas of study. You can get the necessary information from your own aircraft flight manuals or company procedures.

Self Study of Current Aircraft

Get "check ride" familiar with the following:

1) Operational and aircraft limits,

2) Systems descriptions and limitations,

3) Emergency and abnormal checklists, to include memory items,

4) Windshear procedures,

5) Performance, such as range, V-speeds, fuel burn, etc.,

6) Engine description, such as manufacturer, thrust or power, model number, etc.,

7) Anti-ice/de-ice systems, characteristics, capabilities, and limits,

8) APU or EPU operations and limits,

9) Unique characteristics of your aircraft, such as mismatched or asymmetrical elevators of the MD-80 during preflight.

General knowledge

Don't expect that these questions are exhaustive! These are just representative of the ones you may be asked.

What is the main advantage of an APU's centrifugal flow compressor?

Answer: The main advantage is a shorter length compared to the axial flow compressor.

The speed (RPM or percent) of the high pressure compressor of a dual compressor engine is referred to by what symbol?

Answer: The high pressure compressor is referred to as N_2.

Which difference does engine pressure ratio (EPR) measure?

Answer: Engine pressure ratio measures the differential pressure ratio between the compressor inlet total pressure (P_{t2}) and the turbine discharge total pressure (P_{t5}).

What is the primary purpose of the oil-to-fuel heat exchanger?

Answer: The primary purpose is to cool the oil. However, many aircraft also depend on the warming of the fuel in the process to prevent water precipitating out of it and freezing as ice crystals on the fuel filters.

? *Which engine instrument readings will indicate higher than normal if the compressor has damage?*

Answer: High EGT, TIT, or fuel flow are indications of compressor damage.

? *If a turbine engine catches fire during the start cycle, what initial action should be taken?*

Answer: With fire indications during the start cycle, move the fuel control lever to off. Continue motoring the engine to ensure an airflow to clear the excess fuel. If the fire persists, discharge the fire extinguishing agent into the engine.

? *What color identifies hydraulic fluid known as MIL-H-5606?*

Answer: MIL-H-5606 is red.

? *What is the purpose of a hydraulic accumulator?*

Answer: A hydraulic accumulator has two purposes: to store hydraulic fluid under pressure (reserve/backup pressure) and to absorb sudden pressure surges (shock absorber).

? *For a transport jet, when are outboard ailerons normally used?*

Answer: Outboard ailerons are only used at slower speeds to help improve low-speed roll control and stability. Normally they are locked out during high speed flight.

What is the purpose of chines on aircraft tires, and what type of aircraft uses chine tires?

Answer: Chines are deflectors built into the outboard sidewalls of aircraft nose gear tires to deflect water away from the intakes of jet engines. Aircraft with aft mounted engines are candidates for chined nose tires. Since these engines are closer to the fuselage and behind the gear they are more likely to ingest water spray from the nose gear during takeoff and landing, especially as the tail is lower to the runway during takeoff rotation and landing flare.

What is the purpose of fusible plugs in aircraft wheels?

Answer: In many high performance airplanes, fusible plugs are installed as a safety device to prevent tires from exploding after heat buildup from an aborted takeoff or maximum braking effort during landing. During this short time of maximum brake use, so much heat is generated in the brakes that the air in the tires expands enough to create a blowout hazard. However, the heat in the wheel melts the core of the fusible plug and allows a slower and safer deflation.

? *What is the purpose of a transformer rectifier (TR)?*

Answer: Converts alternating current (AC) to direct current (DC).

? *What is the purpose of a rotary or static inverter?*

Answer: Converts direct current (DC) to alternating current (AC).

? *In nicad batteries, describe a thermal runaway.*

Answer: Thermal runaway is characterized by high current and high temperature. If excessive current is drawn from the nicad battery, it starts to overheat. But, as the generator recharges the battery, the battery cells take the higher current which causes additional overheating.

? *What is the function of a circuit breaker in the instrument lighting system?*

Answer: Circuit breakers protect the wiring, instead of the lights, from too much current.

? *Which section of a turbine engine typically provides air for the pressurization and air conditioning systems?*

Answer: The engine compressor section.

Which component of an air-cycle machine (ACM) cooling system undergoes both a pressure and temperature drop of air during operation?

Answer: The expansion turbine. Since high-pressure air from the compressor is routed through the expansion turbine, some energy is used to drive the turbine. Thus, the air expands and results in a drop in both pressure and temperature. The resulting cold air is used for cabin air conditioning.

What is the most likely condition for turbine engine icing?

Answer: Ice is most likely to form in a turbine engine when it is operating at a high speed on the ground. Inlet ice is most likely to form in dry air with temperatures between 5 and 40 degrees Fahrenheit, or in visible moisture with temperatures between 5 and 45 degrees Fahrenheit.

What is the purpose of a CSD?

Answer: A CSD is a constant speed drive for an AC engine driven generator. Its purpose is to control the frequency of the generator to a constant RPM and frequency output regardless of the speed of the engine.

NOTES

Chapter 8

AERO 101

KNOWING THE RIGHT STUFF

In this chapter, emphasis will be on a few basics of aerodynamics and performance. The topics can also be found in the ATP and FEX written study guides for additional study.

What affects indicated stall speed?

Answer: Weight, load factor, and (to some extent) power. At a given flap setting an airplane will always stall at the same angle of attack. The three factors listed above are the only variables that we as pilots can change.

What is the highest speed possible without supersonic flow over the wing?

Answer: The highest speed possible without supersonic flow is called the critical Mach number. This also defines the start of the transonic flight regime, which is typically from Mach 0.75 to Mach 1.20.

Why do most jets have a sweptwing design?

Answer: It gives the airplane a higher critical Mach number, and therefore a higher maximum cruise speed.

What are the disadvantages of sweptwing designs?

Answer: There are three significant disadvantages to sweptwing designs:

1) a reduced maximum coefficient of lift. Thus, most jets employ sophisticated high lift devices to ensure acceptable low takeoff and landing speeds.

2) a tendency, at low airspeeds, for the wing tips to stall first. This results in loss of aileron control early in the stall, and in very little aerodynamic buffet on the tail surfaces.

3) Dutch roll tendency. If a sweptwing jet yaws, the advancing wing is at a higher angle of attack and presents a greater span to the airstream than the retreating wing. This causes the aircraft to roll in the direction of the initial yaw and simultaneously to reverse

its direction of yaw. This roll-yaw coupling is usually damped out by the vertical stabilizer, but may not be adequate for turbulence. Thus, most jets have a yaw damper to help counteract any Dutch roll tendency.

What should a pilot do to maintain "best range" airplane performance when a tailwind is encountered?

Answer: Generally, you should decrease cruise speed with a tailwind and increase cruise speed with a headwind.

Maximum range performance of a turbojet aircraft is obtained by which procedure as aircraft weight reduces?

Answer: As a jet burns fuel, its maximum range can be maintained by climbing to improve the specific fuel consumption and by slowing down to stay closer to the optimum L/D ratio.

Describe the three types of hydroplaning.

Answer: The three types of hydroplaning are dynamic, viscous, and reverted rubber.

- **Dynamic hydroplaning** occurs when you roll over standing water on the runway. Similar to water skiing, the tire forms a bow wave, then jumps up on the "step" where there is no contact with the runway surface. A conventional rule of thumb is that dynamic hydroplaning will start at a speed in knots of 9 times the square root of your tire pressure.

- **Viscous hydroplaning** occurs when you roll over a slick surface on the runway. This may be a dew covering the painted surfaces of the runway or a rubber-coated portion of the touchdown zone of the runway. A slippery surface means less friction and braking ability. Viscous hydroplaning can occur at very slow speeds.

- **Reverted rubber hydroplaning** occurs with a locked wheel skid on a damp runway. Small amounts of water now trapped between the locked tire and runway will be heated by the resulting friction and steam is created. Then, the tire rides upon the "pocket" of steam and melted rubber, with minimal contact with the runway. A notable characteristic of reverted rubber hydroplaning is that the tires will deposit a black gummy substance on the runway.

At what minimum speed could we expect dynamic hydroplaning to start on a nose tire with a pressure of 145 psi?

Answer: Using the formula of 9 times the square root of the tire pressure, and knowing that 12 squared equals 144 (close enough), 9 x 12 = 108 knots.

*As you progress through your takeoff roll,
your airplanes gets a blown tire just as you
reach decision speed, V_1. What do you do?*

?

Answer: This is one of the more exciting
scenarios you could be exposed to on the takeoff
roll. You would have steering or controllability
problems, increased drag or lack of acceleration
while on the ground, potential engine FOD from the
blown tire, possible hydraulic line rupture from the
debris, etc.

Conventional wisdom dictates that a pilot
should continue the takeoff with a blown tire at this
critical point. In this case, it is safer to get airborne
than to try to stop. Braking and controllability are in
question and most of the runway for stopping is
behind you.

Therefore, it is better to get airborne, even if
FOD from the blown tire causes you to lose an
engine, and bring it around the pattern for a
stabilized approach to landing. This way you will
have time to analyze your situation and have all of
the longest runway available for stopping. Don't
forget to leave the gear down since FOD from the
blown tire could interfere with gear sequencing.

Please note that the generic solution I have
offered here is just that—additional or unforeseen
complications could easily alter the decision to
continue the takeoff. Once you decide upon your
course of action, stick with it and have confidence
that you can make it work.

*What are the implications of an abort past
decision speed, V_1?*

Answer: A decision to abort the takeoff roll
after reaching the decision speed invalidates the
planned takeoff data and the protection and safety
factors built into the criteria.

Potential problems are:
1) Stopping beyond the end of the runway
   surface, perhaps off a prepared surface,

2) Hot brakes (including melting fuse plugs
   causing the tires to deflate),

3) Fire due to hot brakes,

4) Controllability problems due to hot
   brakes/deflated tires causing asymmetrical
   drag or steering problems,

5) Increased risk of evacuation for the
   passengers,

6) Increased response time for crash rescue
   teams if the abort results in stopping beyond
   from the normal runway area.

*You are flying an ILS approach. Tower has
reported winds as light and variable. As you
descend below the cloud deck you notice
that the heading of the aircraft is pointed
several degrees to the left of the runway
centerline as you continue to maintain
course centerline and on glide slope. How
will you control the airplane for the landing*

and touchdown for this unplanned crosswind?

Answer: There are two techniques used to decrab the aircraft for landing. The first is to decrab using a cross-control or "slip" method starting several hundred feet above touchdown, depending on the severity of the crosswind. The second technique is to "kick-out" the crab angle during the flare and just prior to touchdown.

The first decrab method is accomplished by simultaneously performing three tasks. As in this example, use the right rudder (1) to align the nose of the airplane with the runway heading while (2) adding opposite (or left) aileron to bank into the direction of the crosswind (to control the sideways drift of the airplane). Use enough bank to move over and maintain runway centerline. At the same time, since these control inputs are creating additional drag, (3) add a small amount of power to maintain the desired approach speed. Maintain the rudder and aileron deflections throughout the roundout, flare, touchdown, and rollout to prevent drift across the runway. In fact, as you slow down crossing the threshold, your control inputs may have to increase in size to maintain a straight track down the runway centerline.

The second method of "kicking-out" the rudder during the flare and touchdown is used more often by heavy aircraft such as the Boeing 747. (This technique is used is to minimize the need for large bank angles at touchdown for aircraft with large wing spans. There is much less probability of striking a wingtip or engine pod as might occur when cross-controlling during the first decrab method as described above.) This technique requires lots of experience, judgment, and timing. As a simple explanation using the question from above, the pilot will wait until crossing the threshold to push the right rudder to align the nose with the runway centerline, while adding a small amount of left aileron to keep the wings level. Maintain this until touchdown. The large amount of inertia of this large airplane will keep the aircraft tracking down the runway centerline for the short amount of time until touchdown. If the pilot makes the rudder input too early, the airplane will start drifting prior to touchdown. If the pilot makes the rudder input too late the airplane will touchdown in a crab. Both errors in timing will make for a rough touchdown.

For the next four interview questions, develop an answer that has both a beginning, a middle, and an end. I find it helpful to visualize the scene in the cockpit, including putting yourself in the captain's seat, to resolve the issue.

What items would you highlight during a crew briefing for a takeoff into known icing conditions?

Answer: Cold weather operations require special consideration in three specific areas: preflight planning, de-icing procedures, and additional checklist procedures.

At operations, I would ensure that I calculated takeoff speeds based upon adverse runway conditions and specific flap settings. As such, I may need to coordinate a change in payload if needed, and I may need to brief special items for the takeoff V-speeds.

At the gate, I would brief the cabin crew on the procedures for de-icing and inform them that the flaps may not be positioned for takeoff till just prior to takeoff, that the first officer will come back into the cabin just prior to takeoff for a visual inspection of the wings, and that it may be necessary to cycle the landing gear once airborne to clear the mechanisms of slush. I would also inform them of an engine run-up just prior to takeoff to clear the engines of ice.

Prior to pushback, I would also brief/review with my copilot special procedures in the following areas:

1) De-icing, visual inspection, engine run-up, holdover time;

2) Taxiway and runway conditions, takeoff speeds, flap setting, engine EPR/N_1, abort consideration;

3) Engine and wing anti-ice/de-ice procedures, bleed air considerations, and use of continuous ignition.

After takeoff and during the climb to cruise altitude, you notice you have smoke in the cockpit. What would you do?

Answer: My initial thoughts are to **fly the airplane**, analyze the situation, and take the appropriate action. In that order.

First, I would engage the autopilot to help maintain aircraft control. Second, I would don my oxygen mask and smoke goggles. Third, I would call for the copilot to run the emergency checklist for smoke in the cockpit while I was flying and talking on the radios.

As soon as practicable, I would request assistance from ATC to make an emergency descent for landing. I would also inform the cabin crew of the emergency, tell them the time remaining till landing, and enlist their help in identifying the source of the smoke. I would also instruct the cabin crew to plan on an emergency evacuation after landing.

Since time may be critical, I would declare an emergency, run the appropriate checklists, and make an emergency descent for landing at the nearest appropriate airfield.

If the smoke continues after landing, I would initiate an emergency evacuation after stopping.

During the enroute descent to landing, your first officer tells you ahead of time that he will "drop the gear at 1,000 feet agl." How would you respond?

Answer: This sounds like a Crew Resource Management (CRM) issue. Several items may need to be addressed and clarified by the captain.

1) Review standard operating procedures. Clarify the need to extend the gear in a timely fashion in accordance with the flight

manual and checklist. Since we all pick up bad habits over time, this may be a good opportunity for the captain to conduct some training for the copilot (or captain-in-training).

2) Clarify with the first officer that you, as captain, expect him (or her) to perform configuration changes and run checklists as called for. The first officer is not to overrule the captain's authority or responsibility to conduct the flight by the rules. Again, this may be another example of a bad habit picked up over time. After all, most guys don't really care, right? This may also be a good time to discuss crew coordination, responsibilities, and expectations.

3) After the flight, discuss with the copilot these two areas from above to ensure that he (or she) is not confused about the proper procedures and crew coordination. And finally if appropriate, let him know how much it is appreciated when he flies "by-the-book."

You are 5 knots slow on final approach, but fully configured and on glideslope. What are you going to do?

Answer: I would immediately add power to regain the proper target speed. Then I would reestablish the appropriate power setting to maintain the increased speed.

Since this 5 knot deviation may have only been temporary, I would continue the approach to landing if I remained stabilized in accordance with company procedures.

If time permits, I would also confirm my actions with the copilot and ask for help in maintaining tighter tolerances on the approach.

Chapter 9

SUMMARY

A llow me to reiterate the three areas of preparation that should supplement this study guide.

- Know your current airplane's limitations and systems.

- Review approach plates and enroute/area charts.

- Schedule a mock interview with qualified and competent airline consultants.

For your own sake, don't leave out any steps in this process of preparing yourself for the biggest job interview of your life!

One word of caution! Everyone seems to know that there is a lot of "gouge" out there on the streets, in the squadron, within your network of flying buddies, on the internet chat rooms, etc. I've run across some misleading information in all those places. **Be very careful of what you accept as accurate!** To put it bluntly, some of the technical interview gouge has been totally inaccurate, only half true, or incomplete.

Therefore, please verify any and all information you receive. It is important that you back it up with source documents.

But, most of all, don't wait till the last minute to get started with your studies, getting your documents and records in order, and scheduling a mock interview. It's best to do these things earlier than at the last minute.

So, good luck! I hope to see you flying the line very soon!

Chapter 10

A NOTE FROM CHERYL A. CAGE

STAYING ON COURSE

Even though answering technical questions in an interview may feel more "familiar" to you, the fact that you are in an environment where people are making decisions about your career can add a different type of stress to the situation. For this reason there are quite a few techniques that we teach applicants to use during the personnel side of the pilot interview that are also extremely helpful when practiced during the technical interview.

Fly The Plane

When faced with an emergency in the cockpit, pilots are taught to never stop "flying the plane." You are instructed to remain focused on the task at hand and not to waste your brain power concentrating on other factors that don't immediately impact the safety of the flight or the solving of the emergency.

It is the same situation in any interview. You must clear your mind and focus only on the question that has just been posed to you. Eliminate from your mind the last question you were asked and the fact that perhaps you stumbled on the answer. In addition, **do not anticipate questions**. Don't use part of your brain to worry about, "What will they ask next?" Concentrate on the question they are asking **now**.

If you are able to "fly the plane" during your technical interview you will be much calmer, and thus, much more able to work through the problem at hand.

Don't Be Intimidated

Part of the pilot selection process is to constantly critique an applicant's self confidence. It is very easy to do that by simply asking an applicant, "Are you sure of your answer?" In a technical interview it is easy to second guess yourself.

There is nothing wrong with taking a moment to recalculate or rethink your answer. But if you are confident of your answer say, "Yes sir/ma'am!"

On the other hand, if you realize that you have made a mistake, don't be afraid to admit your error. "Actually, sir/ma'am, I believe I did make an error. The correct answer is

_____."

Don't grovel or apologize, just give them the correct response.

Take Your Time

Take your time. It is better to take a minute or so to respond and get the answer right, than to answer in 5 seconds and be close but wrong! No one wants to hire a pilot who rushes to judgment, especially when there is time to think through a problem.

Be Confident Through Preparation—
Set A Study Schedule

Confidence can only come through knowledge of a subject. (Have you ever felt confident going into a test when you haven't studied?) Do not wait until the last minute to prepare for *any part* of the pilot interviewing process, technical or personnel.

Set a study schedule for both your technical **and** your personnel interview preparation. Begin your preparation *well in advance of any interviews.* (I have had many clients begin the preparation process as much as a year before any anticipated interviews.)

Through early and complete preparation you will be able to present yourself as the confident, knowledgeable professional that *any* airline would be proud to have flying their aircraft!

Good luck!

Chapter 11

GLOSSARY

Definitions and Abbreviations

AIM: Aeronautical Information Manual

Aircraft Classes: For the purposes of Wake
    Turbulence Separation Minima, ATC classifies
    aircraft as Heavy, Large, and Small as follows:

Heavy: Aircraft capable of takeoff weights of
    more than 255,000 pounds, whether or not
    they are operating at this weight during any
    particular phase of flight.

Large: Aircraft of more than 41,000 pounds
    maximum certificated takeoff weight, up to
    255,000 pounds.

Small: Aircraft of 41,000 pounds or less
maximum certificated takeoff gross weight.

ALS: Approach Light System.

ALSF-I: Approach Light System with Sequenced
Flashing Lights.

ALSF-II: ALS with Sequenced Flashing Lights and
Red Side Row Lights the last 1,000 feet.

ASOS: Automated Surface Observing System.
Reports the same as AWOS-3 plus
precipitation identification and intensity and
freezing rain occurrence (future enhancement).

ATC: Air Traffic Control.

ATIS: Automatic Terminal Information Service.

ATP: Airline Transport Pilot.

AWOS: Automated Weather Observing Station.

AWOS-1: Usually reports altimeter setting, wind
data, temperature, dewpoint, and density
altitude.

AWOS-2: Provides the information provided by
AWOS-1, plus visibility.

AWOS-3: Provides the information provided by
AWOS-2, plus cloud/ceiling data.

AWOS-A: Only reports altimeter setting.

Balanced Field Length: Accelerate-go distance equals Accelerate-stop distance.

CAT: Clear Air Turbulence.

Ceiling: The height above the earth's surface of the lowest layer of clouds or obscuring phenomena that is reported as "broken," "overcast," or "obscuration" and not classified as "thin" or "partial."

CL: Centerline Light.

Critical engine: The engine whose failure would most adversely affect the performance or handling qualities of an aircraft. Note: It is important to recognize that there are two characteristics that are defined here. To simplify the impact of the loss of the critical engine, performance relates to the ability to continue to climb or minimize sink rate. Handling qualities relates to the ability to keep the wings level and the nose pointed straight.

DA(H):   Decision Altitude (Height).

Designated Mountainous Areas: Refer to AIM
Figure 5-6-2 and FAR Part 95. This diagram
illustrates that the majority of the conterminous
United States west of the Rockies plus a section
of the Appalachian mountain area is recognized
as designated mountainous areas.

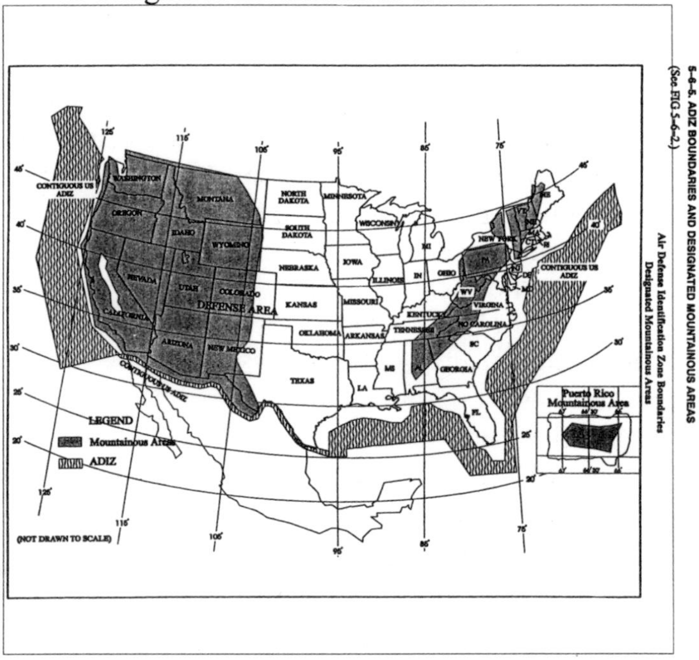

Illustration 17: Designated Mountainous Areas

DH: Decision Height.

DME: Distance Measuring Equipment.

ETA: Estimated Time of Arrival.

ETE: Estimated Time Enroute.

FAA: Federal Aviation Administration.

FAF: Final Approach Fix.

FAP: Final Approach Point.

FAR: Federal Aviation Regulation

FEX: Flight Engineer written exam.

FL: Flight Level

Grid MORA (Grid Minimum Off-Route
    Altitude):An altitude derived by Jeppesen or
    provided by State Authorities. The Grid MORA
    altitude provides terrain and man-made
    structure clearance within the section outlined
    by latitude and longitude lines. MORA does
    not provide for NAVAID signal coverage or
    communications coverage.

    1) Grid MORA values derived by Jeppesen
        clear all terrain and man-made structures by
        1,000 feet in areas where the highest
        elevations are 5,000 feet MSL or lower.
        MORA values clear all terrain and
        man-made structures by 2,000 feet in areas
        where the highest elevations are 5,001 feet
        MSL or higher. When a Grid MORA is
        shown as "Unsurveyed" it is due to
        incomplete or insufficient information. Grid
        MORA values followed by a +/- denote
        doubtful accuracy, but are believed to
        provide sufficient reference point clearance.

    2) Grid MORA (State) altitude supplied by the
        State Authority (read foreign) provides
        2,000 feet clearance in mountainous areas
        and 1,000 feet in non-mountainous areas.

GS: Ground Speed.

GS: Glide Slope

GSIA: Glide Slope Intercept Altitude.

HAT: Height Above Touchdown.

HIRL: High-Intensity Runway Light System.

IAF: Initial Approach Fix.

ICAO: International Civil Aviation Organization.

IFR: Instrument Flight Rules.

ILS: Instrument Landing System.

J-Route: Jet routes designated on high altitude enroute navigation charts.

L/D Ratio: Lift to Drag Ratio.

LOC: Localizer.

M: Symbol for the Missed Approach Point on Jeppesen approach plates.

MAA (Maximum Authorized Altitude):   A published altitude representing the maximum usable altitude or flight level for an airspace structure or route segment. It is the highest altitude on a Federal airway, jet route, area navigation low or high route, or other direct route for which an MEA is designated in FAR

95 at which adequate reception of navigation aid signals is assured.

Mach number: The ratio of true airspeed to the speed of sound.

MAP: Missed Approach Point.

MCA (Minimum Crossing Altitude):   The lowest altitude at certain fixes at which an aircraft must cross when proceeding in the direction of a higher minimum enroute IFR altitude (MEA).

MDA: Minimum Descent Altitude.

MEA Gap: Established on enroute charts to denote a gap in nav-signal coverage.

MEA (Minimum Enroute IFR Altitude):   The lowest published altitude between radio fixes which assures acceptable navigational signal coverage and meets obstacle clearance requirements between those fixes. The MEA prescribed for a Federal airway or segment thereof, area navigation low or high route, or other direct route applies to the entire width of the airway, segment, or route between the radio fixes defining the airway, segment, or route.

METAR (Aviation Routine Weather Report):   New ICAO format for the old hourly surface observations (SA). Refer to Chapter 6 for details of the new format.

MM: Middle Marker.

MOCA (Minimum Obstruction Clearance Altitude): The lowest published altitude in effect between radio fixes on VOR airways, off-airway routes, or route segments which meets obstacle clearance requirements for the entire route segment and which assures acceptable navigational signal coverage only within 25 statute (22 nautical) miles of a VOR. In the case of operations in mountainous areas, 2,000 feet above the highest obstacle within a horizontal distance of 4 nautical miles from the course to be flown; or, in nonmountainous areas, 1,000 feet above the highest obstacle within a horizontal distance of 4 nautical miles from the course to be flown.

MRA (Minimum Reception Altitude): The lowest altitude at which an intersection can be determined.

MSA (Minimum Safe Altitude): Altitudes depicted on approach charts which provide at least 1,000 feet of obstacle clearance for emergency use within a specified distance from the navigation facility upon which a procedure is predicated. These altitudes will be identified as Minimum Sector Altitudes or Emergency Safe Altitudes and are established as follows:

1. Minimum Sector Altitudes — Altitudes depicted on approach charts which provide at least 1,000 feet of obstacle clearance within a 25-mile radius of the navigation facility upon which the procedure is predicated. Sectors depicted on approach charts must be at least 90 degrees in scope.

These altitudes are for emergency use only and do not necessarily assure acceptable navigational signal coverage.

2. Emergency Safe Altitudes — Altitudes depicted on approach charts which provide at least 1,000 feet of obstacle clearance in nonmountainous areas and 2,000 feet of obstacle clearance in designated mountainous areas within a 100-mile radius of the navigation facility upon which the procedure is predicated and normally used only in military procedures. These altitudes are identified on published approach procedures as "Emergency Safe Altitudes."

MSL: Mean Sea Level.

MVA: (Minimum Vectoring Altitude) The lowest MSL altitude at which an IFR aircraft will be vectored by a radar controller, except as otherwise authorized for radar approaches, departures, and missed approaches. The altitude meets IFR obstacle clearance criteria. It may be lower than the published MEA along an airway or J-route segment. it may be utilized for radar vectoring only upon the controller's determination that an adequate radar return is being received from the aircraft being controlled. Charts depicting minimum vectoring altitudes are normally available only to the controllers and not to pilots.

NM: Nautical Mile.

NoPT: No Procedure Turn authorized.

NOTAM: Notices to Airmen.

OPSPECs: Operations Specifications.

PAPI: Precision Approach Path Indicator.

PDP: Planned Descent Point.

QFE: Height above airport elevation (or runway threshold elevation) based on local station pressure.

QNE: Altimeter setting 29.92 inches of mercury. 1013.2 hectopascals or 1013.2 millibars.

QNH: Altitude above mean sea level based on local station pressure.

RAs: Resolution Alert.

RCLM: Runway Centerline Markings.

Route MORA (Minimum Off-Route Altitude): This is an altitude derived by Jeppesen, for use on Jeppesen navigation charts only. The Route MORA altitude provides reference point clearance within 10 NM of the route centerline (regardless of the route width) and end fixes. Route MORA values clear all reference points by 1,000 feet in areas where the highest reference points are 5,000 feet MSL or lower. Route MORA values clear all reference points by 2,000 feet in areas where the highest reference points are 5001 feet MSL or higher.

RVR: Runway Visual Range as measured in the touchdown zone area.

RVRNO: RVR information not available.

SA: Surface Analysis weather report.

SLPNO: Sea Level Pressure information not available.

TAF (Aerodrome Forecast): New ICAO format for the old airport terminal forecast. Refer to Chapter 6 for details about the new format.

TAs: Traffic Alerts.

TAS: True Air Speed.

TCAS (Traffic Alert and Collision Avoidance System): TCAS I provides proximity warning only. No recommended avoidance maneuvers are provided nor authorized as a direct result of a TCAS I warning.

TCAS II provides traffic advisories (TAs) and resolution advisories (RAs). RAs provide recommended maneuvers in a vertical direction (climb or descend only) to avoid conflicting traffic.

TCAS III provides features of TCAS II plus RAs in a horizontal direction (turn left or right) to avoid conflicting traffic.

TCH: Threshold Crossing Height.

TDZL: Touchdown Zone Lights.

TERP: United States Standard for Terminal Instrument Procedures.

TIT: Turbine Inlet Temperature.

TR: Transformer-Rectifier.

V_1: Maximum speed in the takeoff at which the pilot must take the first action (e.g., apply brakes, reduce thrust, deploy speed brakes) to stop the airplane within the accelerate-stop distance. V_1 also means the minimum speed in the takeoff, following a failure of the critical engine at V_{EF} at which the pilot can continue the takeoff and achieve the required height above the takeoff surface within the takeoff distance.

V_2: Takeoff safety speed, a referenced airspeed obtained after lift-off at which the required one-engine-inoperative climb performance can be achieved.

V_A: Design maneuvering speed.

VASI: Visual Approach Slope Indicator.

V_B: Design speed for maximum gust intensity.

V_{EF}: The speed at which the critical engine is assumed to fail during takeoff.

VDP: Visual Descent Point.

VHF: Very High Frequency.

V_{LE}: Maximum landing gear extended speed.

V_{LO}: Maximum landing gear operating speed.

V_{MC}: Minimum control speed with the critical
    engine inoperative.

V_{MO}/M_{MO}: Maximum operating limit speed.

VOR: VHF Omnidirectional Range.

V_R: Rotation speed.

NOTES

Index

References

Reference is made to AIM on Pages:

. . . . 34-35, 49, 51, 56-68, 82, 85, 88, 126

Reference is made to FAR on Pages:

. . . . 35, 47, 49, 64, 71-78, 126.

NOTES

About the Author

Although *Airline Pilot Technical Interviews* is the first book written by Ron McElroy, you can see that Ron is a natural writer. Additionally, his many years as an instructor in the classroom and the cockpit have developed his deep understanding of flying. He is uniquely able to cut through the fog and pass his knowledge and understanding of technical issues on to future airline pilots, having been through the interview process himself a couple of times.

For over 23 years Ron has been flying in nearly every area of aviation possible. He's been an Air Force test pilot at Edwards Air Force Base; a flight and ground instructor for the Air Force, several FBOs, and an aviation college; a charter pilot; a skydive pilot; photo and chase plane pilot; simulator instructor and line pilot for two airlines; and is currently flying for a major airline. Ron has flown 94 types of aircraft in his career, from the Piper Cub to the Boeing 777, and the military T-38 to the C-17.

Ron has always maintained a multifaceted interest in all levels of teaching pilots about the technical aspects of their profession. Armed with that experience, he has provided a tremendous service to those pilots needing just a little help to start new careers as airline pilots.

Ron has consulted with many pilots both before and after their interviews. Feedback from those pilots clearly points out that technical preparation is a key part of the process. Ron gives everyone an afterburner full of mental exercises to help them hone their skills and translate those skills into a successful interview experience.

CAGE CONSULTING, INC.

BOOKS AND CDs

To order call (toll free) 1-888-899-CAGE (2243) or, order online at www.cageconsulting.com

Checklist for Success: A Pilot's Guide to the Successful Airline Interview by Cheryl A. Cage (Revised yearly.)

This is the best, most complete pilots guide to successful airline interviews. A comprehensive, easy-to-follow, positive approach to preparing for your interview. Over 15,000 copies sold through reader referral.

"All the advice I could provide is contained in this book." W.H. Traub, Vice-President, Flight Standards and Training, United Airlines (Ret.) $31.00

CHECKLIST Interactive CD ROM Training Companion. Developed by Cheryl A. Cage

Like being in an Interview Simulator! With Cheryl as your guide you will *see and hear* examples of some of the most commonly made interview mistakes and the positive scenarios you will experience after using this invaluable CD. Includes: Self-Evaluation, Paperwork Presentation, Interviewer Styles, Interview Scenarios, Interview Attire and more! (Suggested to be used after reading *Checklist for Success* (book).) $39.95

PURCHASE the CHECKLIST SET (book and CD) and Save!

Flight Plan to the Flight Deck: Strategies for a Pilot Career by Judy A. Tarver.

Judy Tarver, President of UPAS and former Manager of Pilot Hiring for a major US airline has authored the aspiring professional pilots guide to career planning. *Flight Plan* covers education requirements, building flight time, record keeping, networking and more. *"Seminar-to-go,"* says *Flight Training* magazine. $14.95

OTHER CAREER TITLES

Welcome Aboard! Your Career as a Flight Attendant by Becky S. Bock.

Becky Bock is a flight attendant with USAirways and a former Flight Attendant Interviewer and Inflight Trainer. This book covers everything you need to know to about how to positively impress during the flight attendant interviewing process and what to expect from the flight attendant lifestyle. $14.95

Can You Start Monday? A 9-Step Job Search Guide - Resume to Interview by Cheryl A. Cage

A step-by-step guide to landing the job of your dreams for new graduates and people reentering the job market. Filled with lots of real-life examples and written with a heavy dose of optimism and motivation! Many business colleges use *Can You Start Monday?* in their career search classes. $14.95

Please add $4.00 for shipping and handling for up to three books.

SERVICES

To learn about our Pilot Interview Preparation Services and our Flight Attendant Interview Services please:

Visit our website at: www.cageconsulting.com

Call us (toll free) at: 1-888-899-CAGE (2243)

Or write us: Cage Consulting, Inc., 13275 E. Fremont Place, Suite 315, Englewood, Colorado 80112